POSITIVE INFLUENCING SKILLS

Terry Gillen is a graduate in the Social Sciences from the University of East Anglia and a Fellow of the IPD. He has worked in training for 20 years, the last 10 of them as a consultant, and has gained wide experience within both the public and private sectors. His specialisation is personal skills development for both individuals and organisations facing major change. A freelance trainer and visiting tutor at both Ashridge Management College and Highlands College Management Centre in Jersey, he is also the author of *Assertiveness for Managers* (1992).

POSITIVE INFLUENCING SKILLS

Terry Gillen

INSTITUTE OF PERSONNEL AND DEVELOPMENT

Typesetting by The Comp-Room, Aylesbury
Printed in Great Britain by
The Cromwell Press, Wiltshire

British Library Cataloguing in Publication Data
A catalogue record for this book is available from the British Library

ISBN 0-85292-572-7

**INSTITUTE OF PERSONNEL
AND DEVELOPMENT**

IPD House, Camp Road, London SW19 4UX
Tel: 0181 946 9100   Fax: 0181 947 2570
Registered office as above. Registered Charity No. 1038333
A company limited by guarantee. Registered in England No. 2931892

Contents

Preface   vii

1 Introduction   1

2 Fundamental Principles   10

3 The Core Skills   36

4 Bringing It Together   117

5 Gameplans   136

6 Implementation   206

7 A Few Final Thoughts   211

Further Reading   215
Index   217

As always, to my family

Preface
The Steve Davis Principle

I remember reading in a Charles Handy article that apparently Steve Davis, the champion snooker player, once said that getting the balls in the pockets should not be the main focus of attention for snooker players. The rationale behind the statement is that whether or not the balls go in the pockets is simply *confirmation* that the players have done the right thing with their arms! They will perform better, therefore, if they focus their attention on getting their arms right rather than on getting the balls in the pockets.

It is a concept that transfers readily to the workplace. What we achieve at work is a direct result of what we have done, so we should focus our attention on what we need to do to achieve the results we want, rather than on the results themselves. This may sound obvious, but I come across:

- managers who push their staff towards tougher targets, when they would do better to work with their staff on what they need to do to meet those targets
- salespeople who moan about falling orders, when they would do better to change the way they market and sell
- specialists who criticise line managers for not understanding them, while they would do better to change the way they explain their case.

I recently came across two companies, one large and one small, who decided to produce statements of their mission and values. After much deliberation (and expense) they were ready. The small company pinned their statement to the notice-board while the large one had several thousand glossy booklets printed and distributed to each member of staff. Both companies achieved exactly the same thing: cynicism. Neither had thought through the link between their intentions and the results they wanted to achieve in terms of what people would actually have to do. So it did not happen. Instead, employees saw just one more example of management failing to 'walk the talk'. The Steve Davis principle is not so widely accepted as one might suspect.

I find that when I am running courses or advising people on issues relating to the management of change, conflict resolution, management style, motivation, customer care, quality or whatever, I am constantly drawn towards *behaviour*, what people actually *do*, if the concepts and theories are to have any practical meaning. Behaviour is the link between intentions and results and, unfortunately, it is the link that is all too often neglected.

Something else I have noticed with increasing frequency is a growing need for face-to-face skills amongst almost everyone. As organisations de-layer, people are communicating more, and, as the communication rules of the old 'command and control' structures whither, their ability to get things done with others depends less on their position in the hierarchy and more on their influencing skills. Shop-floor workers are attending meetings, agreeing production schedules and contributing to quality procedures. Specialists, such as finance and marketing people, are having to persuade line colleagues of the value they bring or face being one of the many functions outsourced in the next shake-out. Relationships that were once clear-cut and taken for granted are now subject to new rules and require both new thinking and new skills to be maintained.

Yet most of us have an in-built obstacle to performing better in face-to-face situations. We have a tendency to pigeon-hole information. We feel comfortable if it has a label on it such as 'selling', 'appraisal interviewing' or 'counselling'. Consequently, we do not readily transfer skills and tactics gained in one setting to another. This is a pity because whenever I am giving feedback to people during role-play exercises I find myself highlighting the same faults time and time again, and recommending the same few core skills that would make an immense difference, irrespective of the type of role play being observed.

I also find that if feedback is to be beneficial, it has to pass the TSR Test. TSR stands for That Sounds Reasonable. I have learned that if the feedback I give and the suggestions I make to people – whatever the psychological origins of the feedback and suggestions – do not have the ring of common sense, they are rarely accepted. Even if they are 'accepted' at the time, they are unlikely to make the eventual journey from classroom to workplace. If, on the other hand, they do sound reasonable, they are much more likely to be implemented.

This book concentrates on improving people's face-to-face effectiveness with others. The intention is to help people use their behaviour to link the results they *want* in face-to-face situations with the results they *get* – and it is by no means easy to make the two coincide, especially during times of change.

Like every other trainer I know, I have over the years soaked up a lot of information from conversations, books, articles and many other sources. Sometimes the origins of that information are well known but at other times they are way beyond my recollection. Wherever possible, therefore, when describing other people's work, I have made the appropriate acknowledgement. Should any information have slipped through the net, the lapse was entirely inadvertent.

Having said that, everything in this book has been tried and tested over a number of years on a variety of people, such as managers, professionals, specialists, bankers, scientists and engineers, male and female, young and not so young etc. Those people have come from a variety of organisations public and private, large and small and so on. Everything in this book has passed their TSR Test, as well as my own. The feedback I have received shows that it does make a difference both to people's influencing ability, and to the quality and productivity of the work relationships they enjoy.

There is no doubt in my mind that the messages in this book will help make people more effective at work. Whether or not it improves their snooker is more open to debate.

November 1994

1

Introduction

The ability to influence people, and to do so positively, is something that most of us could do better – and we would be all the better for it.

Generally, it is not something that has been encouraged in us. (Even professional influencers, such as salespeople, do not always do it positively.) Neither our informal education at home nor our formal education at school and work tends to put sufficient emphasis on it. Yet it is a skill that enables us to achieve more when working with other people and it boosts our personal credibility. So what is it? How can you benefit from it? And why is it so important? In this chapter I will address all three questions.

Perversely, it will be easier if the questions are tackled in reverse order. So, I shall begin with my personal view on how people react to social revolutions.

People and revolutions

Two hundred years ago, people working in fields may well have seen friends and neighbours pack their belongings and move to the rapidly growing city to work in something called a factory. They probably thought it unnatural to work all day in one of those places and regarded the migration as peripheral to 'the way things are'. They did not know it, but they were living through what we now call the Industrial Revolution. It seems to be a feature of social revolutions that we fail to see them until long after they have started.

Since the Industrial Revolution we have had the decline of imperialism, the emergence of the service sector, mass production of the silicon chip and the growth of world-wide competition. We have experienced difficulties along the way as former colonies no longer accepted their roles as suppliers of cheap raw materials and eager markets; as we failed to reskill our work-force and direct service organisations into the old industrial heartlands; as computerisation changed the nature of many jobs; and as global competition forced cost-cutting strategies on many organisations with the accompanying, and inadequately termed, 'right sizing'.

We are now experiencing a related revolution. One which is having a fundamental effect on relationships at work and the skills we need to be successful. Far too many people have failed to see that a revolution is taking place and will probably fail to do so until it becomes painfully obvious. Their efficiency, their competitiveness and their people will all suffer.

What revolution?

The drive for efficiency and competitiveness has caused many organisations to adopt concepts such as customer care, total quality, de-layering, matrix teams, re-engineering, empowerment and so on. These concepts are being adopted with similar zeal in the public sector where, in the UK at least, compulsory competi-tive tendering, market testing and contracting-out are forcing commercial realities into hitherto untouched nooks and crannies. These changes share two common features. First, they change the way people work together. Second, they require skills differ-ent from those required to be successful in the past. Together, they amount to a revolution in workplace relationships. Let's take each of these changes in turn.

Not so long ago we lived in a relatively stable environment; customers were not too demanding and workers had minimal ed-ucation. A typical commercial strategy, therefore, was *cost lead-ership*. This entailed deskilling production operations, growing to a size where economies of scale can be reaped, and control-ling workforce activities in detail with a mixture of reward and punishment. In the second half of the twentieth century, at least, rewards were very often based on the assumption of long-term employment. They included short but frequent steps up the pro-motion ladder, a pension and benefits (unrelated to the work that was done) such as private health insurance or sports facilities. Punishment often centred on alienation from the group either by dismissal or transfer to the organisational equivalent of Siberia. Characteristics such as these give rise to a culture where the management style is one of command and control: your superiors know best, because they are the ones responsible, and it is unsafe to challenge either them or the organisation's norms and values. Workforce alienation from the task is accepted.

Today, however, we live in a relatively unstable environment; customers are very demanding and workers are better educated. A typical commercial strategy is to *specialise*, to compete on *quality* and *responsiveness* or both. Organisations following such a strategy require innovation, individual and team responsibility, and constant learning. So as well as remuneration, rewards tend to centre on satisfaction from the work itself and from the synergy between people. Such characteristics give rise to a 'team leadership' style of supervision and a natural sharing of activities that were once the sole preserve of management. Job analysis at Nissan UK has confirmed, for example, that shop-floor workers there are routinely performing tasks that not so long ago would have been well within the managerial domain. Challenging the status quo is not only accepted, it is encouraged. Workforce ownership of the task is not only expected, but initiatives like customer care and TQM (Total Quality Management) simply do not work without it.

That, in essence, is what the revolution is all about. The past model of successful organisations is being replaced with a new model of success. The old one was characterised by large enterprises, tall organisational structures, superior and omnipotent management and an alienated workforce. The new one is characterised by small units, flat structures, open, informal and participative team leadership and an involved workforce. The workforce *has* to be involved because, with modern business initiatives, success is just as dependent on a delivery van driver or a telephone sales clerk as it is on a senior manager.

This commercial reality is changing the way people at work relate to one another. In the old-model organisation, managers needed skills enabling them to command and control, to motivate, make decisions and solve problems etc because these activities were their sole preserve; workers needed technical skills (that is, the ability to keep their heads down and get on with the job). In the new-model organisation, however, *everybody* needs skills to enable them to work as a team, to solve problems and to make decisions jointly, to be creative and, above all, to communicate.

It is true that I have presented this information in terms of extremes, but I have done so to emphasise certain points:

- Successful organisations of the future will not look like successful organisations of the past. And the pace and magnitude of that change qualifies it to be classed as revolution rather than evolution.
- Most of the initiatives being adopted by organisations today depend for their success not on senior decision-makers but on the people who not so long ago were thought of simply as order fodder.
- If people are going to 'sign on' to these commercial imperatives, they need to be managed in such a way that employers can involve their hearts and minds and not just exploit their labour.
- To involve the hearts and minds of an educated workforce with high expectations managers need to move away from an authoritarian style to a participative one. (There are risks in such a move but they can be minimised with the appropriate attitudes and skills.)

Your own organisation will probably be somewhere between the two extremes described above. I say this because, on the one hand, companies relying solely on a cost leadership approach to their competitive strategy tend to suffer at the hands of their more modern-thinking competitors and, on the other hand, companies such as W Gore & Associates and Ricardo Semler's Semco are still very few and far between.

Those readers who have not yet come across these two companies should be aware that they are organised very fluidly with no managers in the traditional sense of the word, with incredibly open communications and even more incredible freedom of action. Many employees, for example, are allowed to set their own salaries and holiday entitlements; they also determine which of their team-mates get hired, fired or promoted. Much to the surprise of many traditionalists in management, both companies are very successful. If you want to find out more, you will probably enjoy doing so: Tom Peters (with Nancy Austin) describes Bill Gore's approach to business, along with that of many other like-minded managers, in *A Passion for Excellence* (London, Collins, 1985) and Ricardo Semler has responded to the interest in his company by writing *Maverick* (London, Century Business, 1993).

If you are between those two extremes (of old- and new-model organisations), you may well be unaware that we are in the middle of a revolution and so not appreciate just how fundamental the need to change really is.

People who fail to see a need to change are usually so wedded to the status quo that they effectively filter information, disallowing anything that contradicts their view of reality and emphasising anything that supports it. In their view the Gores and Semcos are one-off oddities that 'wouldn't work here', and the crises that genuinely require authoritarian solutions strengthen resistance to change. Where a customer-care or TQM initiative founders because management behaviours fail to change with it, the supporters of the status quo do not see a reason to spur those changes on; rather, they see 'proof' that these new-fangled techniques are just a flavour of the month and hope that senior management will eventually come to their senses. Such managers would do well to ask the question, 'What's in it for me?'

What's in it for me?

The problem with social revolutions is that, from the individual's perspective, they tend to happen too piecemeal and too slowly for anyone to be certain what is happening. We know there are changes afoot, but we work within an organisation and feel we have to gear our pace to what feels comfortable there. Learning more positive influencing skills, however, is one area where you can safely steam ahead.

Whether you are a manager or a specialist, consider the nature of *authority* at work. It comes from three sources:

● first, your position in the organisational hierarchy. A manager, for example, has more clout than an assistant manager but less than a senior manager. Higher grades have more formal power than lower grades.

- second, your technical knowledge. In a discussion about computers, the representative from data processing normally has most authority; if the conversation switches to advertising, the marketing representative has most; when the topic is job evaluation, the personnel specialist takes over and so on.
- finally, your personal credibility. This is not something the organisation bestows on you, neither is it something you pass an exam in: it is something people feel about you. Whether they feel you have it or not will depend primarily on the way you behave towards them. If they feel you do not have it, they will be likely to disregard your point of view, pay lip-service to your demands and show you little loyalty. If, on the other hand, they feel you do have it, they will be more inclined to respect you, to listen to you and to follow your leadership.

So, which of these three sources of authority is the most important? I would suggest that position in the hierarchy is not so important these days partly because, increasingly, we show less respect to authority figures and partly because as organisational structures get flatter an individual's position in it no longer inspires the awe it once did. Technical knowledge is also on the wane as computer terminals, networks and empowerment spread information. That leaves a gap which personal credibility is expanding to fit and, as I said earlier, whether people feel you have it or not depends primarily on the way you behave towards them.

Learning face-to-face skills that leave people feeling good will improve your personal credibility. That will in turn improve your chances of getting things done, of building good relationships and of being noticed by more senior management. So, whether you are aware of the revolution and want to be part of it or whether you are still waiting to see what happens in your organisation, improving your face-to-face skills can only be of benefit.

What are positive influencing skills?

They are non-manipulative, persuading behaviours. They enable you to achieve more with other people in such a way that they feel good about the interaction with you.

They are vital for modern organisations. After all, if managers have to rely less on their position in the hierarchy and more on their personal credibility, if specialists have to rely less on their technical knowledge and more on their personal credibility, if achieving results relies more on the active involvement of the workforce rather than on their passive acceptance of orders, everyone will need better face-to-face skills.

As managers are so central to many organisations, as they can determine how other people feel and think, let's take them as an example. If, in modern organisations, managers are spending less time giving orders, checking that procedures are being followed and controlling what their staff get up to – what are they doing? One would hope that they are:

- instilling the right values in people
- agreeing targets with them
- giving productive feedback
- coaching people
- helping people capitalise on learning opportunities
- resolving differences of opinion
- facilitating two-way communication.

All of these activities require skills that have little to do with the traditional view of motivating down the line; they have instead a lot to do with influencing other people.

Here is another example. At one time, a typical training manager organised courses in response to what senior managers said they wanted, and paid for them from the training manager's central training budget. That same training manager is now likely to be in a meeting, persuading the same senior managers to spend some of their limited budget to meet the development requirements of their staff when the senior managers would rather spend it on something of more tangible and immediate value.

A final example: in old-model organisations, a senior manager might call together a number of specialists and tell them what he or she wants them to do. In a new-model organisation, this manager would describe what needs to be achieved and ask the specialists to consider how best to achieve it. They might well have different views but, through a process of discussion, they would between them arrive at solutions they could all support.

Summary

- The old approach to commercial success, while wholly appropriate to the situation that existed a few decades ago, has now passed its 'sell by' date. The new approach to commercial success is one of responsiveness and organisational agility. Initiatives such as customer care, TQM, empowerment etc are aspects of this new approach.
- A significant characteristic of the new approach is that these initiatives only work with the active involvement and support of the entire workforce. Commercial success is now dependent on people who, not so long ago, were thought of simply as order fodder. Companies need therefore to enlist the hearts and minds of their employees, not just exploit their labour.
- Involving all strata of employees requires a participative rather than an authoritarian style of management. This is just as well. First, because better-educated employees with higher expectations from work are less likely to tolerate an authoritarian culture. Second, because multilayered management, producing little that customers actually pay for, are so expensive that delayering has become essential in many organisations – even in the public sector, where commercial values and practices are being adopted.
- A participative style of management requires new skills not just of managers but of everyone. Greater participation means more communication, more discussion, more open disagreement and a greater need to *influence* rather than tell – because the former will capture people's motivation while the latter will just antagonise them. Such influencing needs however to be positive rather than manipulative.
- These changes are so significant that the history books will probably regard them as revolutionary. One of the problems with social revolutions, however, is that they are easier to spot with hindsight than when you are actually living through them. This is partly because most of us have an emotional attachment to the status quo and partly because change, especially where not everyone else is going along with us, can feel risky.
- Acquiring more positive influencing skills is however totally risk free, and indeed beneficial. It changes the way you behave

with other people and that changes the way they feel about you. Your *personal credibility* improves and, whichever type of organisation you are in, that can do you only good.

But why *influencing* skills?

One last point, you may be asking yourself, is, 'Why *influencing* skills? Why not just face-to-face skills in general?' Here's why. There are two reasons. First, most of us feel comfortable when information is neatly pigeon-holed. We tend to do the same with skills. We will readily relate to selling skills, selection skills, appraisal skills, counselling skills, negotiating skills and so on. In my experience as a skills trainer, however, there are only a few face-to-face skills – we simply use them in different ways in different situations. So it is more learning-efficient, and less repetitive, if we concentrate on acquiring the skills than on the situations in which we use them. Second, whether you are appraising, coaching, reprimanding or counselling, you are in effect influencing. You will be attempting to alter someone else's perceptions, views, beliefs, attitudes, decisions etc. Influencing skills form a common theme throughout most face-to-face situations in which your personal credibility can be affected.

Preview

Having established, I hope, just how important positive influencing skills are to you, we had better get on and look at them. Before we can do that, however, there are certain fundamentals that we need to cover. They will be dealt with in the next chapter.

2

Fundamental Principles

It will, I hope, come as no great surprise to anyone to learn that our beliefs, values and attitudes affect our behaviour. Put in the context of influencing skills, if you believe that your staff are there to be exploited you will probably have no qualms about influencing them manipulatively. If on the other hand you believe that they have a right to be treated as intelligent adults you may still try to influence them, but you are likely to do so in a more open and honest manner.

The techniques you will learn from this book are based on certain beliefs about people and about what constitutes effective or ineffective influencing. So before we look at the skills we need to look at those beliefs to ensure that you and I are on the same wavelength, as it were; or, at the very least, so that you can appreciate the reasoning behind the skills I am advocating. As these are the principles on which the skills are based I have called them fundamental principles.

In this chapter we will first gain an overview of the principles and then consider each of them in detail.

Overview

The fundamental principles are that when trying to influence someone:

1 *we make better progress if we 'pull' gently at their pace rather than try to 'push' hard at ours*. Far too often we work on the assumption that just because we can see the logic in our case then other people will too. This tempts us to move at our pace, to present information in our own terms, and even to use coercive tactics (however mild) when faced with what we perceive as obstinacy. Even if we 'win' the results are often only temporary and the side effects unwanted. We achieve more,

therefore, when we 'meet' other people where they are and encourage them gently to move in the direction we want them to go.

2 *we achieve better results if we* **involve** *them in the discussion rather than allow them to be passive.* Some people just like the sound of their own voices while others believe that if they let the other person talk they will lose control and be unable to influence them. If we involve someone the right way, however, we actually improve our chances of successfully influencing them. 'The right way' means encouraging them to think through our argument in such a way that they arrive at the conclusion we want (which is, of course, subject to point 3, below).

3 **persuasion** *produces better results than manipulation*, yet it is easy to confuse the two. Persuasion, in this context, is based on approaches that respect the other person, make it easy for them to see your point of view, and invite them to accept your way of thinking. Manipulation, on the other hand, is based on a kind of stealth whereby the other person is tricked into accepting your way of thinking. This can even happen unintentionally where, for example, people inadvertently use tactics that make the other person feel guilty if they do not comply.

4 *it is better to think in terms of* **behaviour** *than personality.* As human beings we find it very easy to label people. We observe their behaviour and draw conclusions about them, their state of mind and personality. We can label them lazy, obstinate or uncooperative. Yet all we really know is their behaviour; everything else is pure conjecture. We may be correct but it is still guesswork, whichever way we choose to dress it up. By focusing on their behaviour, however, we can do something very useful: we can ourselves adopt behaviours that will produce a better than even chance of their behaviour changing to what we want. As our own behaviour is all we can realistically control, starting there is usually the best place.

5 *we do well to remember that the* **beliefs** *affecting our behaviour are probably different from other people's.* That is important because people's beliefs and assumptions are often so deep-rooted that we cannot hope to influence them at a superficial level: we have to dig deeper. So, as a general rule, if we seek first to understand we will know better how to make ourselves understood.

So, there is an overview of the five fundamental principles on which the influencing skills are based. How do you feel about them? My experience of running courses on positive influencing skills is that although most people have never actually thought about such skills in the past, once they have heard about them they feel as if long-held but unco-ordinated thoughts have just crystallised into a cogent whole.

We will now move on to examine each of the skills in turn. If you are in full agreement with them, the following pages will expand your appreciation of them. If on the other hand you are not wholly convinced about them the following pages may help to convince you.

'Pull', don't 'push'

Introduction

Most people would agree that if we coerce, manipulate or trick someone into doing what we want, we are unlikely to get totally satisfactory results. If on the other hand they do what we want voluntarily, the results are likely to be better. This section describes the rationale behind this principle and how too many of us, unfortunately, do not put it into effect.

Example

Imagine a situation in which a salesman is trying to sell something to a prospective customer. The salesman knows that the product is right for the customer; he can see exactly what benefits it will bring. He also knows the price is fair and that if the customer uses the product correctly it will pay for itself in less than a year. The fact that the salesman knows all these things is, however, immaterial. It is the *customer* who has to know them because it is the customer who has to make the decision whether or not to buy.

How easily the customer comes to the same conclusion as the salesman depends on many factors, such as whether the customer has the same depth of understanding as the salesman, is a willing prospect, or is being 'cold called' and so on. What we can say is that if the salesman assumes that just because he can see the logic of his argument the customer will do too, he may soon be disappointed!

Yet this assumption is a mistake that many of us make too often. It is easy to forget that when trying to influence someone we are in a similar position to the salesman. We may not be selling something in the literal sense of the word but we still want someone else to 'buy into' our way of thinking – which is another way of saying that we want them to agree with us genuinely and voluntarily. Hence they, and not just we, have to see the logic of our argument.

Counter-productive behaviour

The consequence of not recognising this fact is that we can behave in counter-productive ways:

- We talk too much at the other person, believing that the weightier our case the more likely they are to come to our conclusion.
- We talk in terms that make sense to us but do not necessarily make sense to them. The use of jargon is a good example of this.
- We are less inclined to listen to their point of view. We hear what they are saying but when their viewpoint differs from ours we make little attempt to understand. Instead we counter with our own viewpoint.
- We use prescriptive language such as 'should', 'ought' and 'can't'. To us it may be obvious that the other person ought to do something, but a statement such as 'What you ought to do is . . .' will be less productive than a question such as 'What would be the effect if you . . .?' (In fact prescriptive language is usually counter-productive because it often antagonises. It is too reminiscent of the way parents and schoolteachers used to talk to us as children so that, even though we may not realise it, when another adult speaks to us that way we tend to resent it and become defensive.)
- When faced with someone who does not see what, to us, is

13

blindingly obvious we can jump to the conclusion that the fault is theirs and attempt to overcome their obstinacy or stupidity with manipulation or even coercion. We can attempt to 'out-logic' them (trap them with their own defence), make them feel guilty if they do not comply, or make them fearful of the consequences of non-compliance. All of which produces someone with the grudging acceptance of a conscript rather than the motivation of a volunteer.

Consequences

Talking at the other person, using terms they may not understand, not listening, using prescriptive language, and being downright manipulative may on occasions deliver the agreement we seek. Our victory is likely to be short-lived, however, as the other person will probably become more and more uncomfortable with the outcome – which will only produce problems in the future. They will gradually withdraw their co-operation, not do the task as well as they could have done it, fail to understand some vital aspect, refuse to use their initiative, work to rule, and so on. All of which will make our early success seem somewhat sour.

Why do we get it wrong?

It sounds, I hope, fairly obvious when explained this way, so why do we not follow this principle as often as we could? The main reasons are described below.

- We rarely see a good role model. We have grown up with parents who tried to alter our behaviour by talking at us, schoolteachers who tried to teach us by talking at us, and managers who tried to motivate us by talking at us – rather than by discussing with us and trying to see our point of view.
- We make the same assumptions as poor salespeople. We assume that just because we can see the logic of our case the other person will see it too.
- We are not aware that our behaviour tends to trigger a response in the other person and are therefore unaware that the

unproductive response from the other person is actually being triggered by ourselves!

What does *pulling* mean?

'Pulling' means using the sorts of behaviours that will cause the other person to think through the situation so that they can appreciate and accept the point you are making. Behaviours associated with 'pulling' include seeking information, questioning to help the other person 'rethink' their position, building on their suggestions and open, relaxed body language. It is the opposite to 'pushing', which means using the sorts of behaviours (usually manipulative and coercive) that leave the other person with no choice but (grudgingly) to accept the point you are making or totally to reject both it and you. Behaviours associated with 'pushing' include asking leading and evaluative questions, meeting another's proposal with a counter-proposal, and closed or invasive body language. The net result may appear the same but – and it is a big 'but' – the former outcome is more likely to be sustainable whereas the latter outcome may suffer all the consequences referred to above.

We achieve more when we 'meet' the other person where they are and 'pull' them gently, with the appropriate skills and at their pace, in the direction we want them to go. It may help to think of attaching a thin thread to the other person: pull too hard or too suddenly and the thread will snap and you will have lost them. Pull gently and you will be able to lead them in the direction you choose.

The 'pulling' approach requires both patience and skill. It is not loved by people who are too busy or too self-important! My reaction to such people is twofold. First, if you cannot find time to do the job properly can you find time to do it twice or three times? Because that may be the price of not successfully influencing the other person first time around. Second, if what you want is not *dependent* on the other person why are you trying to influence them in the first place? So you might as well influence them effectively. If you are one of these people you may find it useful to read the Introduction again!

The basic message is this: *encouraging someone to 'buy in to' your way of thinking is easier if you 'pull' gently at their pace rather than 'push' hard at yours.*

Involvement is more effective than passivity

Introduction

To have people involved rather than passive is sometimes a difficult principle to grasp because it appears contrary to much of our experience. As I mentioned above, most of us have had experience of parents, teachers, salespeople and managers who have attempted to exert influence by talking at rather than involving us. The rationale for hogging the discussion has a spurious logic to it: if we let the other person express views contrary to what we are trying to achieve that will surely make it more difficult for us to achieve it. In fact, the reverse is true: if the other person has views contrary to what we are trying to achieve we had better hear them; to do otherwise will make it more difficult to achieve our goal. Their objections are there whether we hear them or not. If we do not hear them we have little chance of addressing them; but if we do hear them we will see what obstacles there are and how best to tackle them.

In the 1960s and 1970s Neil Rackham of Huthwaite Research Group conducted a major piece of research relevant to this point. Using behaviour analysis methods to observe professional influencers (in this case, negotiators) he found, amongst other things, that those negotiators who were effective involved the other party significantly more than those who were ineffective.

Example

Think of the salesman example we used a moment ago. If the customer does not want to buy the product is it because it is too expensive, too big, too small, the wrong colour, or because the customer already has one, or what? Without this vital information the salesman does not know which features and benefits to emphasise.

Imagine a shift supervisor who wants to introduce a revised

roster. She believes it will overcome a lot of the problems staff have had in travelling to work and will make the service much more attractive to customers. Yet her staff seem very lukewarm about the idea. Should she emphasise the easier travelling, stress the need for a competitive advantage in the current climate, or what? If the problem that the staff foresee relates to personal security when the dark winter evenings come or with difficulties over child-care arrangements the supervisor can talk until she is blue in the face but her influencing power will be severely diminished and remain so until she involves her staff in the discussion.

Benefits

That is one benefit of involvement – we find out which obstacles need to be addressed.

Another benefit is that we find out what will attract the other person to our proposition. Again, a sales example provides a good illustration. If a car salesman is trying to sell a car one potential buyer might be attracted by its nippy performance, another by its frugal running costs, and yet a third by the image created by its TV advertisements. The salesman will not know what to emphasise unless he involves the customers. Let's take this a stage further to illustrate a third benefit.

Encouraging someone to 'buy into' our way of thinking is easier if they can visualise what it will mean to them. So the car salesman might ask the potential customer interested in running costs what he will do with the money he saves with this model; he might ask the potential customer interested in image what the car will look like parked on her drive, or what her friends will say when she parks in the office car-park. The supervisor trying to introduce the new roster might ask her staff how they would use the time they would save travelling, or what the improved customer-care points would do to their quarterly bonus.

Those involved in management (and that is anyone from a team leader to a chief executive) might like to know that this visualising concept fits neatly with Charles Margerison's *common vision*. While at Cranfield School of Management Margerison analysed managerial influencing styles and found that one of them, which he referred to as common vision, was a powerful oratory tool favoured by impressive public speakers and charismatic leaders. It centres on using descriptive language so that an audience can *visualise* what the speaker is advocating. Watch for it the next time you see a politician addressing a party conference or a group of potential voters; you will see a lot of it.

Another benefit to 'involving' can best be described with an example from a finance company where I had a consultancy assignment. The incident happened shortly before my assignment began and was described to me by one of the clerical officers. Apparently the former London regional office was becoming too small for the number of people employed and so the company decided to look for new premises. At this time, however, central London office accommodation was outrageously expensive. Senior management therefore decided to relocate to one of the new office developments being built on the south side of the River Thames on the sites of old warehouses. The office was prestigious to look at and comfortable to work in. For the managers who drove to the office there was no problem. For the clerical staff who used public transport and who liked to do some shopping during their lunch-breaks, however, there were big problems. The journey by public transport was longer and less 'comfortable' (in a personal security sense) and they were too far from the large shops to visit them at lunch-time. They were, therefore, very unhappy. What they really disliked, however, was not being consulted about a decision that was to have a major and detrimental effect on them. One of the clerical staff put it to me like this: 'We're not fools, Terry. Had we been given the facts we would probably have come to exactly the same decision. What we don't like is them [senior management] making a decision that affects us without even involving us. It's created a lot of bad feeling. Quite a few people are looking for other jobs.'

The message is a simple one. People prefer to be involved in what affects them; they do not like being presented with a *fait accompli*.

Why do we get it wrong?

For the same reasons as in the previous example: lack of good role models and incorrect assumptions about what influencing is really all about.

What does involving mean?

Just that. Make it a two-way dialogue, not a one-way mono-logue. Use skilful questioning to:

- find out what you need to know. Try questions such as, 'How do you feel about that suggestion?' or 'Why is that a problem for you?', or 'What would you do if you had to make this decision?' They will uncover a lot of information.
- help the other person visualise what your suggestion will mean to them. For example ask, 'What would you do with that extra time?', or 'With Christmas coming soon what would the extra bonus payment mean to you?'

Sometimes it helps to think of a *ratio of talking* between you and the other person. In a disciplinary interview you might need to do 70 per cent of the talking; in an appraisal discussion only 40 per cent; and when counselling only 10 per cent. (We will go into questioning in much more detail in Chapter 3.)

The basic message is this: *if you help someone 'see' what your suggestion means to them you are more likely to be successful in influencing them.* The objections that this process may raise exist whether you know about them or not, so you might as well uncover them in order to decide how to tackle them.

Persuade, don't manipulate

When introducing the five principles earlier in this chapter I described manipulation as a kind of stealth whereby the other person is tricked into accepting your way of thinking. Manipulation can be intended or unintended; although I suspect that readers of this book are more likely to have carried out the latter rather than the former type, it is worth examining both.

Intended manipulation

This is the sort of manipulation that can be experienced with aggressive insurance salespeople, double-glazing salespeople etc. Its intention is to use spurious logic to paint you into a corner, as it were, so that your only rational way out is to sign their contract. It is characterised by a combination of closed questions, not listening, sometimes interrupting, and by putting words into your mouth that are later 'used in evidence against you'.

Example

– Now then, Mr Smith, when did you last review your life insurance?

– About 10 years ago – I think.

– That's quite some time, Mr Smith. Are you aware of what even modest rates of inflation can do to the value of money over that sort of period?

– Well, I can't say I've given it that much thought really. Your colleague said it would be adequate for at least 15 years.

– I'm afraid he's no longer with us. But can I assume that you love your family, Mr Smith?

– Of course, but –

– And that you would be devastated to think of them struggling financially if anything happened to you?

– Yes, but we –

– And then there are the school fees. Have you separate insurance on the school fees?

– No. I thought –

– So after inflation and school fees have decimated your insurance there won't be much left. I suggest that if you really love your family you take a look at our new Peace of Mind Plan. I think it's just what you need.

It is possible to use similar tactics with people at work, especially if they are more vulnerable, or junior, to you.

– Wendy, that report I asked you to do: I've had to bring forward my trip so I'll need it by tomorrow morning. OK?

– Tomorrow morning! I'll never get it finished in time.

– I'm afraid you'll have to. I need it.

– But you said you also wanted the product launch information available by then as well.

– Then you'll just have to do both.

– But –

– Don't you realise that we're all under pressure?

– Yes, but –

– And did you or did you not tell me that you were a hard worker?

– Yes, but –

– And at your last appraisal did you or did you not tell me how ambitious you are?

– Yes, but –

– So the answer is surely, 'Yes, it will be done.' Isn't it?

Intended manipulation is unpleasant. It justifiably attracts a range of adjectives from dishonest to bullying. It leaves the other person feeling cheated, hard done by and resentful. And it destroys your personal credibility!

Unintended manipulation

This also uses spurious logic and closed questions to 'paint you into a corner' but involves less aggression. People who try to influence this way are usually unaware that they are guilty of manipulation. They have probably never been taught to be open and honest when making a request and so have grown up relying on subtle manipulation.

Example

This is a real-life example. It concerns a computer operator who was asked to stand in for the shift supervisor and was paid an allowance accordingly. Several months later there was a reorganisation and the post of shift supervisor was abolished. There was therefore no post for the computer operator to stand in for. Due to an oversight, however, the salary allowance continued to be paid. Eighteen months later the anomaly was spotted by someone in the personnel department who confirmed with the computer department manager that the allowance should be stopped immediately. All the computer department manager had then to do was to tell the computer operator the bad news. The conversation went like this:

21

– . . . so when we abolished the shift supervisor post we should also have stopped the allowance. I'm sorry but I'm afraid we're going to have to stop paying it with immediate effect.

– Why should I get a pay cut just because we no longer have shift supervisors?

– It isn't a pay cut as such. It's just that we'll no longer be paying the allowance.

– Well, it'll feel like a pay cut to me. I'm relying on that money to pay my mortgage. I've quoted it to the bank manager as part of my gross earnings.

– Well, I'm afraid I can't really –

– I may not get the mortgage now. What's my fiancée going to say?

– I'm sure that –

– One minute everything's going all right, then suddenly someone pulls the rug out from under you. How would you like this to happen to you?

– I wouldn't, but –

– You're my manager. I thought you were there to support me.

– Well . . . perhaps I could have a word with personnel.

Note the spurious logic employed by the computer operator: calling the loss of the allowance a pay cut, bringing his fiancée into the equation and, the trump card, implying that the manager has let him down. All this logic is designed to make the manager feel responsible for the computer operator's position (unenviable though it is) and guilty for not having a magic wand. Yet on examination the logic is this: 'I didn't check my salary details with you before giving them to the bank manager – that's your fault; my fiancée will be very upset – that's your fault; you wouldn't like this to happen to you, yet you're making it happen to me – that's not fair; your acting correctly over my pay is the same as a withdrawal of your support for me – managers *should* support their staff.'

It is unlikely that the computer operator is trying to manipulate his manager deliberately. He is understandably upset (to the extent that he forgets that, from another angle, he has been receiving money for over a year to which he was not entitled) and so applies the 'logic' as he sees it.

You probably come across other examples daily. The manager who normally lets a colleague use her secretary whenever she is busy, but who cannot on one occasion, will be greeted with the observation, 'But you always help me out when I'm busy.' The implication is, 'Why have you suddenly changed? People should be consistent.' The manager who delegates a report to a member of staff, and subsequently tells him that he has just promised it will be ready two days early will plead, 'But I've promised: you're not going to make me break a promise, are you?' The implication is 'I've made an unrealistic commitment, but it will be your fault if I have made myself look stupid.' The member of staff who seeks clarification about a hastily delegated task will be told, 'I hope you're not going to make me late for my meeting.' The implication is, 'You're responsible for my poor time management.'

Time and time again we fall for the spurious logic yet at the same time we know that the accompanying feelings of guilt, responsibility, awkwardness etc should not really be part of the equation. By the time the cerebral dust settles we know that we have been duped and feel bad about it.

Why do we manipulate?

We learn from a very early age that some feelings and emotions are pleasant and that others are uncomfortable and best avoided. Parents, older siblings and other authority figures seem adept at using this fact to influence our behaviour. With carefully chosen words and body language they can make us feel good, bad, happy, sad, and so on. As is often the case it is the negative feelings that have the greatest impact on us and so give rise to the most memorable learning experiences. We learn that feelings of guilt, embarrassment etc make us take action to avoid those feelings. We experiment to see if we can make such manipulation as we experienced work for us too and, gradually, we incorporate the appropriate tactics into our growing repertoire of how to deal with other people. That repertoire we take with us into adulthood.

How does persuasion differ?

Whether manipulating or persuading, you are trying to influence someone else so that they will do what you want. The difference is that manipulation uses tactics designed around spurious logic, negative feelings, or both, while persuasion – as I use the word – relies upon openness and honesty. Even allowing for the fact that some people may not want to be persuaded, persuasion is likely to prove more productive than manipulation. Manipulation will give rise to bad feelings about you and what it is you want the other person to do; their commitment to the course of action will diminish as it gradually dawns on them that they have been manipulated. On the other hand persuasion, because it uses openness and honesty which show respect to the other person, makes it easy for them to appreciate your point of view. If they accept your invitation to agree with you their commitment is likely to be sustained into the future. (The skills described in Chapter 3 will enhance your persuasive ability without the need for recourse to manipulation.)

The basic message is this: *persuasion, using approaches that respect the other person, will produce better results than manipulation.*

Think behaviour rather than personality

Introduction

Old habits, so they say, die hard and one of the habits that most of us have acquired is a tendency to label people. We observe their behaviour and, from it, draw conclusions about their personality, their state of mind and their motives. We may be right in our assumptions, but we may also be wrong.

This point needs to be stressed. That is exactly what they are – assumptions – and if we are not careful we are in danger of formulating our approach towards someone else based, in the final analysis, on guesswork. And that means we could get it woefully wrong.

Example

A recent and comparatively young recruit to a section has been promoted section supervisor. This is her first management role and the promotion has come as a surprise to everyone. Most people thought the job would go to the longest-serving member of the section, a middle-aged woman, who acts as a bit of a mother figure for the younger members of the team. The section needs quite a shake-up and so the new supervisor has a lot of initiatives to implement. In section meetings the older woman keeps finding fault with most of the proposals made by the new supervisor.

What should the new supervisor do – have the older woman reprimanded, treat her badly in the hope that she will apply for a transfer, ignore the problem and hope that it will blow over, or have it out with her once and for all? Well, it all depends exactly what the problem is. All we know at this stage is that the older woman keeps finding fault with the new supervisor's proposals. We can however assume from this observation that she is being obstinate because the younger woman got 'her' job! She may indeed be being obstinate or – and it is a significant 'or' – she may simply be a perfectionist, or may have a high need for security, or may be trying to make sure that the fledgling supervisor does not make a mistake, or any one of several further alternatives. But if the new supervisor's tactics for dealing with the 'obstinate' member of staff focus solely on tackling her obstinacy, they will probably prove wholly inadequate. We, like the new supervisor, need therefore to resist the temptation to fix on people unhelpful labels based on assumptions, and to seek a more productive alternative.

What is the alternative? To stick with what we know and to recognise a simple fact: what we know is what we can observe. In this example we know that the older woman is finding fault with the supervisor's proposals. That is what we know and that is what we have to deal with. The simple fact is that a certain behaviour in one person triggers a certain behaviour in another person or, more precisely, different types of behaviour in one person will trigger different types of behaviour in another person with a reasonable degree of predictability.

Here is a quick example. Let's say that you and I are in conversation and you are being very passive. As the purpose of this fictional conversation is for me to obtain information from you, your passivity is unhelpful to me. I could label you shy, uncooperative, selfish (and they are just some of the polite labels), or I could adopt a behaviour myself that will probably trigger the behaviour I want from you. That is I can *ask you a question* because I know from research that, when asked a question, there is a 60–90 per cent chance that you will answer it. When you have answered it I can then probe more deeply, build on what you have said, and so on. I have resisted the temptation to make an assumption and label you. Instead I have altered my behaviour to trigger in you the behaviour I want.

This is the gist of what Peter Honey calls *behaviour modification*. Peter is a very well-known consultant psychologist. Along with several colleagues he has observed and recorded which behaviours in one person will trigger which behaviours in another. They have been pooling information for over 10 years now and so their data base on this subject must be one of the largest in the world. Their findings are broadly summarised in Table 2.1.

What does Table 2.1 mean in practice? It means that if you adopt certain behaviours you can be reasonably sure of the response you will trigger in the other person. And as some behaviours are more positive than others it makes sense to use those that are likely to trigger a positive response than those that are likely to trigger a negative response.

So:

If you want someone to	the best behaviour from you is to
– propose ideas	seek ideas
– make suggestions	seek ideas and support them
– build on ideas	build on ideas yourself
– support your ideas	build on their ideas and make suggestions
– seek clarification	build on their ideas and clarify your point
– clarify their point	ask them to!

But beware:

if you	the other person may just
– disagree	disagree back
– propose ideas	state difficulties
– state difficulties	do almost anything!

Table 2.1
Behaviour triggers and responses

Behaviour trigger from you	Response from the other person	
	Highly likely	Quite likely
Behaviour relating to the generation of ideas:		
Seeking ideas (asking people for ideas)	Proposing ideas	Making a suggestion
Proposing an idea (voicing your idea as a statement)	Stating difficulty; Supporting your idea	Seeking clarification
Making a suggestion (voicing your idea as a question)	Supporting you	Stating difficulty; Seeking clarification; Building on your idea
Reactions to what other people have said or done:		
Building on their idea (developing someone's idea)	Seeking clarification; Supporting you	Building on what you have said; Stating difficulty
Supporting them (agreeing with what someone has said)	Clarifying/explaining; Proposing; Suggesting	None
Disagreeing with them	Clarifying/explaining; Disagreeing with you	Seeking clarification
Stating difficulty (pointing out the problems in what someone has said)	None	Clarifying; Proposing; Disagreeing; Seeking clarification; Seeking ideas; Suggesting
Behaviours relating to clarifying and discussing information:		
Seeking clarification	Clarifying	Stating difficulty; Supporting
Clarifying your point (giving extra information, explanation etc)	Clarifying their point; Seeking more clarification from you	None

27

Yet most people still find it almost irresistible to disagree instead of, say, seeking clarification, to propose ideas instead of suggesting them, and to state difficulties instead of clarifying their point.

The exceptional benefit of this alternative approach is that it encourages us to avoid any natural tendencies to say simply what *we* want without finding out what the other person wants, or to be negative. Instead it encourages us to concentrate on behaviours that will trigger positive responses in the other person. There is no guarantee those positive responses will be exactly what we want to hear but if people explain why they do not agree with you rather than just say 'That's a load of rubbish' you stand a much better chance of influencing them. If you are interested in looking at Peter Honey's work in more detail, I would recommend *Improve your People Skills* (London, IPM, 1988) and *Problem People* (IPM, 1992).

Why don't we do this more often?

Our brains are very efficient recognition machines. For example you may see someone regularly on your way to work but not actually know them. Then, on holiday, in unaccustomed surroundings where you did not expect to see them and when they are wearing totally different clothes, you catch a brief glimpse of them – and instantly recognise them. An actor you have seen on television may be in a drama requiring heavy make-up and period costume, yet there is something about the eyes, the voice or a gesture that you recognise.

We can be just as quick at recognising situations. We know that if a motor mechanic assessing our car sucks in air through his teeth while rubbing his chin we should add 20 per cent to the estimate given over the telephone. We know that if someone gives us multiple excuses why they cannot help us as promised their reasons are not that genuine. We know that if a colleague stands up as we enter their office they are hoping we will not stay long.

We have a natural disposition to 'recognise' things and to label them accordingly. It is one of our most useful learning mechanisms as we grow, helping us get to grips with the world. Without it we would have to relearn too many things too many times. But there is a downside, which is threefold. First, we need very little information for the recognition process to begin, which makes it easy for us to jump to incorrect conclusions. Second, labelling someone lazy, for example, is very comforting because it absolves us of the need to do anything about it. After all, 'You can't change someone's personality, can you?' Third, once it is labelled we tend to filter information accordingly, accepting that which supports the label and discounting that which contradicts it. We also translate information according to our predefined views. So, going back to our new supervisor, a searching question from a 'nice' member of staff in response to a proposal might strike her as 'a very good question' whereas the same question from the 'obstinate' member of staff might seem 'typically awkward'.

In summary, it is *behaviour* that is the problem. It does not matter whether someone has negative attitudes until they behave; their attitudes do not affect us until they behave; we do not even know about the negative attitudes until they behave. Allocating labels describing their personality will therefore never be as helpful as accurately describing their behaviour. So the basic message is *think in terms of behaviour rather than personality*. That way you stand a better chance of positively influencing other people.

Seek to understand, *then* to be understood

Introduction

Here is an analogy. Imagine trying to give someone directions over the telephone. You both have a map in front of you. Your map is up to date and their map is old, showing none of the new roads, by-passes, one-way systems or pedestrianised areas. Neither of you realises that you have different maps. Can you imagine the confusion? A similar thing happens when two people who each have different beliefs about a topic are talking. Neither understands, or is understood by, the other.

Example

Imagine a situation where a new customer has placed a trial order. If the order is handled efficiently there will be a lot more business in the pipeline. Dispatch is running late, so to meet the promised deadline the clerk responsible for the order intends to come in voluntarily on a Saturday morning, which is not usually a workday, and she needs help from a colleague. The clerk believes in doing a job well and takes personal pride in overcoming challenges. She also understands the competitive nature of the business and so appreciates the importance of this trial order. Her colleague, on the other hand, believes that management will exploit any sign of enthusiasm and that a fair day's work for a fair day's pay requires strict limitations on unpaid overtime. The two clerks are new to each other and do not yet know what 'makes the other tick'. The conversation might go like this:

– I'm way behind on this order. I'm going to have to come in tomorrow morning to finish it. How do you fancy helping me?
– Tomorrow morning? Who sanctioned that?
– No one.
– You won't get paid for it.
– I'm coming in voluntarily.
– You must be mad. You wouldn't catch me doing that.
– I won't get the order out in time otherwise – and I need help.
– So send it out late. It won't matter.
– But I don't want to.
– A proper goody two-shoes, aren't you?
– But I helped you the other lunch-time.
– That was a lunch-time. Take my advice: give them an inch and they'll take a yard. Don't come in tomorrow unless you want to come in every other Saturday from now on.

The clerk has failed to persuade her colleague because she did not recognise that their beliefs were so different.

Consequences

Our beliefs affect the way we behave. If you believe that teamwork and co-operation are important your behaviour will be different from the person who believes that you have got to look out for number one. If you believe that position in the organisational hierarchy should command respect you will probably be at odds with someone who has a more casual approach to boss–subordinate relationships. If you believe that perfection is required in even the smallest tasks you will have problems delegating to a member of staff who thinks that 'good enough' is the best use of time.

Our beliefs tend to lie very deep within us. Often we do not even think about them, but they dictate our behaviour nonetheless. Similarly we rarely open them up for discussion. So when we have a difference of opinion with someone we inadvertently keep the conversation at a superficial level and fail to address the real differences between us. Arguing with a junior manager about how frequently staff appraisals should be done is pointless if you believe in the benefits of regular, informal appraisal and he has experience only of formal annual appraisals that went wrong. You think appraisals are a good thing, he thinks they are not a good thing. You have to resolve that difference before you can discuss frequency if you want to influence the junior manager to accept your way of thinking.

Beliefs about what?

How far do you need to go when considering someone else's beliefs? Do we need to become amateur psychologists and probe their feelings towards their mothers? Of course not, but remember that beliefs run pretty deep. During our formative years we develop lots of beliefs about ourselves, other people, what satisfactory relationships and acceptable behaviour look like, and so on. Some people will believe that disagreement is a sign of an unsatisfactory relationship and so will try to avoid it, while others will believe that disagreement is a normal part of a healthy debate. Some people will believe that their role in life is to be the underdog and will accept poor treatment as the norm, while others will be acutely aware of the thin end of any wedge that might undermine their rights. Some people will believe that courtesy and respect are inalienable human rights, while others will think that being the boss entitles them to be rude if that gets the job done.

We all have beliefs about ourselves, other people, situations, and the way things *should* be. Those beliefs tend to vary from person to person but because we tend to group together with people who share similar beliefs about the way things should be we tend not to notice the differences until we come across people whose beliefs differ markedly from our own. When a sleepy rural village becomes the venue for a free rock concert, for example, we witness what the press often describes as a 'clash of cultures'.

The differences do not have to be so marked, however, to cause problems. When times are stable, organisations develop a culture, and relevant beliefs become common to those who work there. When times change rapidly, however, people's beliefs get out of synchronisation. One person wants to adhere to procedures, while another feels it is more acceptable to take short cuts to achieve results. One person still clings to the comfort of status-related power, while their colleagues are shaking off the reserved parking spaces and managerial dining rooms. One manager sees staff as a resource with which to get the job done, while others see staff as the people they help to get the job done.

It is especially when resolving differences of opinion that beliefs are important and it is during times of change that differences in beliefs cause problems, because our old assumptions and understandings do not always prove appropriate to the new situation. Just like using an out-of-date street map. This point becomes particularly significant when you consider the amount of change that has happened and will continue to happen in the world of work.

Thinking along these lines can make you more tolerant of other people without compromising on critical issues. It can make you selective about the issues you feel require attention. It can also encourage you to listen genuinely – a behaviour that, in my experience, never fails to enhance someone's personal credibility.

The basic message, therefore, is: *seek first to understand and you will know better how to make yourself understood.*

Summary

- Our beliefs about influencing affect the way we attempt to influence people, so it makes sense to ensure that those beliefs are sound.
- My beliefs about influencing are based on five fundamental

principles. They are shown in Table 2.2.

- The principles are moral, in that by following them you respect other people's rights. They pass the TSR Test (see page viii). Putting them into practice will encourage and facilitate effective influencing behaviours.

Table 2.2
The five principles – summary

The principles	Characteristics
1. 'Pull', don't 'push'	• It is not just we who need to see the logic in our case but the other person has to as well. • We need to move the discussion at their pace, not ours.
2. Involvement is more effective than passivity	• Involve the other person – don't 'steal' the conversation. • Encourage them to 'think it through'. • Encourage them to 'visualise' what we are advocating.
3. Persuade, don't manipulate	• Respect the other person. • Watch for, and avoid, unintentional manipulation.
4. Think behaviour rather than personality	• Observe behaviour; avoid labels. • Because behaviour is observed, not assumed, our influencing tactics will be more accurate. • If we choose our behaviour carefully it can trigger predictable responses in the other person.
5. Seek to understand *then* to be understood	• Beliefs affect our behaviour. • Beliefs about the way things should be vary from person to person. • In times of rapid change, beliefs get out of synchronisation. • Probe to uncover them.

Pause for thought

Before we move on, you may like to pause for thought and consider to what extent these principles show themselves in your current behaviour. In Table 2.3 are 10 questions. Answer them honestly and see what they reveal about you.

Table 2.3
Fundamental principles – questionnaire

When trying to influence someone, how often do you:	(*Tick the appropriate box*)		
	Rarely	Sometimes	Often
1. feel they are being deliberately obstinate or stupid or slow?	☐	☐	☐
2. use prescriptive language, making suggestions sound like instructions?	☐	☐	☐
3. find it odd that they cannot see the benefits in what you are suggesting?	☐	☐	☐
4. find yourself talking more than the other person?	☐	☐	☐
5. find it is quicker to 'browbeat' or 'out-logic' the other person to get what you want?	☐	☐	☐
6. use jargon that is not necessarily shared by the other person?	☐	☐	☐
7. find yourself attaching labels such as 'obstinate' or 'stupid' to the other person?	☐	☐	☐
8. feel as if you just do not understand 'where the other person is coming from'?	☐	☐	☐
9. engage in debate during which you promote your own case and deliberately avoid finding out more about the other person's?	☐	☐	☐
10. find yourself increasingly at odds with the prevailing views of other people?	☐	☐	☐

For those who have completed the questionnaire:

- if you ticked 'rarely' for most answers, well done (although you might want to ask someone else for their opinion to check you are not being too generous to yourself)
- if you ticked 'sometimes' for most answers, you will find the core

skills useful in helping you adopt more of a 'pulling' style of influencing

- if you ticked 'often' for most answers, well done for honesty! It is worth asking yourself, however, to what extent you agree with the content of this section. If you are not converted to this way of thinking, exactly what are your objections? Do they pass the TSR Test? Do other people agree? How would truly effective influencers you know score on the questionnaire? What do they do that is different from you?

Preview

In Chapter 3 we are going to look at five core skills that will enable you to put the principles into practice.

3

The Core Skills

In this chapter we are going to examine five core skills that will help you put the five fundamental principles into practice. They are the sort of skills that you might come across (and probably have) on any interpersonal skills, interviewing, selling, or negotiating course. What I shall be doing in this chapter however is not to give you a full, 'textbook' account of each skill but to focus on those aspects which I have found from years of running face-to-face skill courses, will make a real difference to your influencing skills.

Note

Please do not make the assumption that because there are five principles and five skills then the first skill relates to the first principle, and so on. That will give you the wrong 'frame of reference' for this chapter. *All five skills are relevant to all five principles.* They are introduced below and subsequently described in more detail.

Probing and listening

Sometimes these two skills are dealt with separately. In my experience, however, they are two sides of the same coin. It is impossible to listen *actively* without knowing how to probe, and probing is of little value if you do not know how to listen to the responses. This probably accounts for the fact that I have never met anyone who was good at probing who was not also a good listener, and vice versa. Probing and listening are central to involving people, encouraging them to think through what you might be suggesting, and appreciating how it would affect them and, of course, seeking to understand before you seek to be understood.

Getting on the same wavelength

This is a skill that makes it easier for you to 'pull' rather than 'push' because it helps synchronise the other person's thoughts with yours, and so speed up the conversation. It lessens the likelihood that they will misinterpret what you are saying and so fail to 'keep up with you'.

Persuasive selling

I come across some people on courses who recoil from the thought of learning some sales skills. Their definition of a salesperson tends to be someone who persuades you to part with money you don't have for something you don't want. Their experience tends to be of manipulative salespeople. Not all salespeople are like that, however. Some have tactics to identify what is important to you and help you see the connection between what you need and what they are selling. In short, while we may not want to employ these tactics in exactly the same way as a salesperson we can learn from them and use them to help us 'pull' rather than 'push', to involve the other person, and to seek to understand.

Awareness of body language

Body language is important for several reasons. First, most people are unaware of their body language. Hence a lot of it comes out unedited. By observing it we can gain useful information about what they are thinking or feeling. Second, we need to control our own body language. This is partly to ensure that it supports, rather than contradicts, what we are saying and partly because, with some gentle 'stage management' of our body language, we can boost our chances of influencing someone. Most of us can therefore benefit from an improved awareness of body language.

Assertiveness

While this is a whole topic in its own right there are certain aspects of assertiveness that I have found essential when coaching people (even successful senior managers) in positive influencing skills. Some of those aspects give us skills to help make us more persuasive, to focus on behaviour rather than personality, and to improve our tolerance where underlying beliefs may differ. Some of the aspects are tailor-made, moreover, to protect ourselves from the manipulative tactics that other people may try to use against us.

In addition to these skills, I shall also describe some real 'no-noes' – behaviours and tactics that may seem useful at first glance but which invariably prove counter-productive.

Probing and listening

I sometimes refer to probing as the universal spanner in your interpersonal skills tool-kit. It is without doubt the most useful and versatile skill to possess. Its benefits are numerous.

- It involves the other person. As long as you ask the right sorts of questions the other person is more or less guaranteed to respond.
- The responses to your questions provide you with information.
- By asking questions to which the person responds (remember *triggers* and *responses*?) questioning keeps you in control of the pace and direction of the conversation.
- It presents you as authoritative. Oddly, someone who asks incisive questions comes across as more knowledgeable and credible than the person who answers them.
- Questioning buys you thinking time. While the other person is talking at about 165 words a minute you can be thinking at thousands of words a minute without necessarily losing concentration.
- Questioning can signal your thoughts without your actually stating them. At times this can be more useful than being direct. For example if you disagree bluntly with someone's proposal they may react negatively with a consequent adverse effect on the conversation. On the other hand, by asking, 'What makes you think I'd agree to that?' you *signal* that you

do not readily accept what they are proposing while, at the same time, finding out some useful information *and* keeping the conversation moving.

● Finally, you are perceived as someone who is interested in the other person, fair-minded, and satisfying to deal with.

These are the real and tangible benefits of probing – if you do it effectively. To help you, here are descriptions of different types of 'probe'. I have divided them into three categories: those that are nearly always useful and so can be used freely and confidently; those that can be unproductive if used incorrectly (they have a more precise use and so need more thoughtful handling); and finally those that rarely produce worthwhile results and are best avoided.

The most useful types of probe

Open question   An open question is one to which it is difficult to reply with 'yes' or 'no', such as, 'How do you feel about . . .? or 'In what way . . .?'. They tend to get the other person talking, providing valuable and genuine information. They show that you are interested in the other person and their situation. They also encourage a ratio of talking in favour of the other person, so they feel they are making a big contribution to the conversation. There is no guarantee of this, however. Shy people can still find a way to give a closed answer to an open question. A little later in this section I will show you how to combine different types of question to encourage even the shyest person to talk.

Reflective question   When reflecting, you send the other person's words back to them. If you have never come across reflecting, this may sound odd. So here is a short example to illustrate reflecting probing, and then I will describe its uses. The example concerns a colleague with a problem who approaches another colleague for help.

– Have you got a minute, Jean?
– Yes. What can I do for you?
– Well, I'm not sure how to begin.
– It's a bit tricky?

– Yes. I've been offered promotion to head Customer Ser-
vices and I'm not sure about it.
– It's got you confused?
– I'll say. I want the job but . . . well . . . I'm just not sure.
– The job has advantages and disadvantages?
– Yes, it's a good career move and the extra money will be
great but it's the hours I'd have to work.
– The hours are a problem?
– Yes. I've got a young family, you see, and I'm not sure
about collecting them from school. I don't know what arrange-
ments the school makes for working parents who can't get there
at normal going-home time.
– If the school has facilities to look after the kids there is no
problem but if it doesn't you'd have to find an alternative?
– That's right . . . I suppose the first thing to do is to speak to
the school and then, if they can't help, to check out alternatives.
Jean, you've been very helpful. You've helped me think this
through. Thanks.

In reality Jean made no contribution to the conversation
other than to reflect back what her colleague had said. The effect, however, was to encourage the colleague to think through
her problem, put it into some sort of perspective, and generate
alternatives herself.

Behaviour in helping situations has been studied in detail by
the American psychotherapist Carl Rogers. He observed that
there are five behaviours we tend to use. The first is *evaluating*:
we make a judgement about what we have been told. The second
is *interpreting*: we make assumptions about what we have been
told without checking facts. The third is *sympathising*: we offer
sympathy but no concrete assistance. The fourth is *probing*: we
seek more information. The fifth is *reflecting*: we return the
words to the sender. According to Carl Rogers, most of us have a
tendency to evaluate, interpret and sympathise rather than to
probe or reflect, yet it is these two behaviours (and in a helping
situation the second particularly) that have the most potential for
real and lasting help. So Jean could have responded by:

Evaluating: I'd turn it down if I were you. It's not
worth the hassle.

Interpreting: Ah, that's because you're torn between your desire to get on in your career and your traditional role as a mother.

Sympathising: I know. It's not easy being a working mother, is it?

Probing: What are the main reasons for your confusion?

Reflecting: It's got you confused?

As we saw from the example it was reflecting that encouraged the colleague to think through the problem for herself. That produces a real and lasting benefit – the solution is 'home-grown' and the colleague is more likely to be committed to seeing it through than if Jean had just given her a solution 'on a plate'.

Although reflecting is most commonly used in counselling situations it has other applications too. When staff are being coached, for example, reflecting encourages them to think through issues for themselves, to consider the consequences of proposed action, and to develop their own solutions. When conducting a selection interview, reflecting encourages the interviewee to provide more and 'deeper' information. For example:

– And when my boss was in hospital I ran the department.
– You had sole responsibility?
– Not at first. The divisional manager insisted I clear everything with him but when he saw that I could handle it, he let me get on with it.
– He gave you complete freedom?
– Yes, for all routine matters like work scheduling, budget control and staff recruitment, but if I wanted to fire anyone or make any capital expenditure I had to let him know.
– You just informed him?
– No, I had to make a proper case to him, but in the six months my boss was in hospital the divisional manager accepted all my recommendations. That's why I want this job, you see. I think I've proved myself, but now that my boss is back from hospital my authority is back to what it was before.

Even in general conversation, the effect is the same – more information that goes a little bit deeper.

41

Hypothetical question A hypothetical question is one that asks someone to respond to a potential or fictional situation. It is best illustrated with some examples, which is also a convenient way of indicating when it is most useful.

The first example concerns a *selection interview*. When interviewing applicants for a job we need quality information. We need to know what the interviewee is really thinking, what they really know and how they would tackle real-life problems. Interviewees however want to present themselves in a good light and so tailor their responses to what they think we want to hear. Hypothetical probes help us obtain quality information without giving interviewees any hint of how we define that quality.

An interviewer who wants to assess an interviewee's approach to leadership, for example, might ask the following hypothetical probe. 'Let's say you take over a team of 20 clerks in the telephone orders department of a large sales company. The clerks have previously had a very procedures-oriented, authoritarian boss who ruled with a rod of iron. Morale is poor and productivity is declining. There are three unfilled vacancies because nobody wants to work there. What would you do in the first three months to rectify these problems?' You have given no hint of the answer you expect and so are likely to receive a genuine answer. You will be able to tell a lot about the interviewee's knowledge and experience from what he or she says. What would *you* do, for example? Assess all the clerks' knowledge and skills? Group them into two or three smaller teams and inject a degree of friendly competition between them? Interview them to uncover the hygiene factors and rectify the problems one by one? Reassess their targets and present them anew as an incentive rather than a threat? Or something else? You could probably also tell a lot about the interviewee from the extra information he or she requested before answering – about the age range, sex, and length of service of the clerks, about how are they targeted, assessed and remunerated, what training have they had, and so on.

The use of relevant hypothetical questions in selection interviewing (where, incidentally, they are sometimes called 'scenario questions') not only produces valuable information but also makes the interview a more stimulating and satisfying process for interviewees. That is important because as you are likely to reject more candidates than you accept it is better to let all interviewees go away having enjoyed the interview as much as possible and feeling as if they have been treated fairly.

The second example concerns *coaching*. Coaching is not about teaching someone how to perform a task to your satisfaction. It is about *helping someone learn* how to perform a task and, because learning is a cerebral process, the more we make them think the better. Hypothetical probes make people think. So as an example let's say a manager is coaching a member of staff to take over her role in a regular interdepartmental meeting. Part of the coaching session might go like this:

– OK, if you deliver our proposal like that, the finance manager might react negatively. If you were in charge of finance, what would be your concerns?

– Oh . . . let's see now . . . I suppose I'd want reassurance that expenditure is still under control.

– Good. So how can you provide that reassurance in your opening remarks?

The benefit of using hypothetical probes in coaching is not just to make people think now but to encourage them to think in the future. Learners work things out for themselves. That makes the learning more memorable and more satisfying. That encourages learners to try it for themselves in the future.

The final example concerns *influencing*. If, say, we want to ask someone to do something and we feel they may not be too keen on our proposal, we have a choice. We can ask them directly, 'Will you do this?', which may trigger the negative response we predicted, or we can ask them obliquely with a hypothetical question:

– John, how would you feel if I asked you to do this?
– I'd want a very good reason why.
– OK, let me explain.

The hypothetical nature of our request means that John feels less threatened by it and, in effect, tells us what we have to do to win him over. All in all John is considering our proposal in a more dispassionate and objective manner than he may do otherwise. He also lets us know what he is thinking. This increases our chances of success. This is not manipulative, by the way. It is simply a way of ensuring that communication is open and contains fewer obstacles than it might do otherwise.

The pause There are two points to make when considering the pause as a method of probing. First, people tend not to like silence during a conversation and will fill it if the silence goes on too long. Second, during a conversation we give other people visual clues, usually with the eyes, that say, 'I'm just about to finish talking and it's your turn next.' (As a matter of interest these visual clues are absent during a telephone conversation, which is why there is sometimes a gap of a second or two between one person ending a sentence and the other person beginning one, and also why it is easy unintentionally to interrupt the other person when they have only paused for breath. Similar problems arise when two people are talking face to face but both are wearing dark glasses.)

You can combine these points to encourage someone to go on talking. They add something to the conversation by giving you some information, for example. You say nothing but look at them, opening your eyes slightly wider and perhaps making the kind of encouraging noises we make when listening ('Mmm', 'Yes?', 'Uhuh'), or inclining the head forward slightly. The other person will then very probably elaborate on the information they have just given you.

Probes that need thoughtful handling

Closed questions Some people learn on courses that open questions are good and closed questions are bad. That is like saying that hammers are good and screwdrivers are bad. If you have ever tried to remove a screw with a hammer you will know how incorrect that statement is. It is the same with open and closed questions: they are simply tools designed for different jobs. I have included closed questions in the 'careful handling' category, however, because it is all too easy to use them incorrectly.

The problem is that our brains work incredibly fast – much faster than the speed of speech coming from the person to whom we are listening. It is easy therefore for our minds to run ahead and to ask questions that check what *we* are thinking rather than find out what the *other person* is thinking. Let's return to our coaching example. During the debrief after the meeting, when the member of staff tells the boss how she responded to the finance manager's questions the boss might ask one of two questions: 'Did you say that because you weren't sure of the answer?' or 'Why did you say that?' The first question is closed and invites the member of staff to confirm what is in the *boss's* mind. The second question is open and invites the member of staff to explain what is in *her* mind.

With the open question there is a very good chance that the boss will get the information she seeks. With the closed question that chance is much smaller. Furthermore, open questions send messages that say, 'I'm genuinely interested in what's in *your* mind; I'm listening.' Closed questions send messages that say, 'I'm more concerned with what's in *my* mind; I'm not listening.'

So why am I advocating closed questions at all? First, they are a great way of checking information, which lets us know how to proceed. If the debrief on the meeting goes like this:

- Did the finance manager behave as predicted?
- Exactly.

you will want to handle the conversation one way. If it goes like this:

- Did the finance manager behave as predicted?
- Not at all.

you will, no doubt, want to handle it differently. These examples occur at the beginning of a conversation. You may also want to check at the end of a conversation. If we revisit the selection interviewing example the interviewer may round off one section of the interview with:

- Just let me check something. On his return from hospital did your boss make any allowance for the fact that you had been running the department for six months?

Second, closed questions are often easier to answer than open ones and so can be used to encourage a shy person to 'open up'. An example appears shortly.

45

Forced-choice questions A forced-choice question is a variety of closed question and so all the pros and cons mentioned above apply here too. It is a bit like a question in a test or questionnaire with a multiple-choice answer. You select the correct answer or the one that is closest to how you would like to respond. We fall into the trap of using forced-choice questions for exactly the same reasons as we fall into the trap of using closed questions: we think ahead and ask the other person to confirm what is in our minds instead of trying to find out what is in theirs. The difference is that we often start with a nice open question but then spoil it by giving the other person a choice of two answers. For example 'How did you feel when that happened?', which is a genuinely open question, becomes 'How did you feel when that happened . . . were you concerned or just plain angry?' As with closed questions we know that the person asking the question is more concerned about what *they* are thinking than what the *other person* is thinking – unless, of course, the question is being used to check or confirm something, or is being used to encourage a shy person to talk.

Here is an example that combines closed and forced-choice questions. Imagine a manager conducting a routine appraisal with a shy member of staff. As you read it, look at how the initial open questions produce minimal response and how the manager then employs closed questions to get the conversation moving by teasing information from the member of staff.

– How do you feel you've performed in the last six months?
– All right.
– How would you describe your performance?
– OK.
– Would you say you've improved?
– I hope so.
– In every aspect of your work?
– I don't know.
– What about the way you deal with customers. Is that better or worse?
– Better . . . I think.
– I agree. You seem more confident. Why is that?
– I know the products better now. And telephone techniques. That course you sent me on taught me a lot. And Jean: she's

been coaching me. And I've been taking the manuals home in the evenings to make sure I understand them.

In this example, the initial open question, contrary to what many people are taught on courses, produces a closed answer, so the manager paraphrases the question and repeats it. This tactic usually produces something – but not in this example. So he then asks a *closed* question and, being easier for a shy person to answer, produces a small response. The manager then asks a *forced-choice* question (again, something else people are usually taught to avoid) but, as with the closed question, it is reasonably easy to answer and so receives a useful response. Having warmed up the member of staff, the manager then tries another open question which finally produces valuable information.

Unproductive probes

There are two main types of probe that rarely, if ever, produce positive results and are best avoided. They are used most often when people are trying to 'push' rather than 'pull' and they leave the other person with the feeling that they are being manipulated.

Leading questions   A leading question is one that tells the other person how you expect or how you prefer them to answer. So 'How do you feel when that happens?', which is a genuine open question, becomes 'You don't like it when that happens, do you?'; 'What are your views on this proposal?' becomes 'Am I right in assuming that everyone agrees with this proposal?' Although there are occasions when leading questions can be used successfully to open a conversation (such as when a child falls over heavily and the parent asks, 'That hurt you, didn't it?') it is really more of a statement than a genuine inquiry. Also whatever it is that we are referring to has to be obvious (such as the graze on the child's knee). Otherwise, leading questions are at best presumptive and at worst downright rude. So even if you want to use one genuinely, say, to open up a conversation with a very shy person, you are on safer ground if you ask an open question, reflect, or use self-disclosure (which is covered in the next core skill).

Evaluative questions   An evaluative question is heavily laden with comment. 'How long are you going to cling to those out-dated views?' is just another way of saying, 'I think you're way out of date.' 'Isn't that rather a naïve way of looking at it?' is just another way of saying, 'I think you're being naïve.'

Evaluative questions come across as manipulative. If we think the other person is out of date or naïve why not say so directly? Or why not state that our views differ and ask the other person to explain the basis of their views? All we do with an evaluative question is antagonise them; they are likely to counter-attack or withdraw from an active part in the conversation, depending on how aggressive or submissive they are.

At this stage you may be saying to yourself, 'But that's exactly the way television and radio interviewers question people, and they don't have any trouble getting the other person to talk'. So let me make a few points. First, TV and radio interviewers often present the sort of questions that are in the minds of the public. Second, they sometimes want to be provocative. Third, they are usually interviewing someone who is more than willing to talk. In fact the interviewer's problem is often to try to get the interviewee to stop talking, or at least to talk in answer to the question. My advice therefore is not to take TV and radio interviewers as an example of how to do it!

Some types of question are therefore better avoided; some can be productive if used with care; and others can be used freely and productively. But if you are going to probe you need to listen to the answers.

Listening

There are several points I want to make about listening. The first is that we like listeners. We feel good about them because they make us feel good. Whenever I have asked people to list the qualities of the boss they have respected most, listening has always been in the top three. Whenever I have asked people to list the qualities of their best-ever boss, colleague, subordinate, friend, or neighbour, listening has always figured high on the list. The second point is to reinforce what I said earlier. Probing and listening are two sides of the same coin. To be good at one you need to be good at the other. This is because listening is an *active* process, not a passive one. (I will explain that shortly.) The final point is that if you *look* as if you are listening the other person will be encouraged to talk more (according to one piece of research, about twice as much as if you do not look as though you are listening). In this section, therefore, I want to describe what active listening involves.

Active listening   Listening can be both active and passive. To distinguish between the two it will be helpful if we understand more about what we mean by listening. We tend to think of it as a single behaviour yet, in reality, for those of us not gifted with mental telepathy it is more of a sequence of events. This is what we are doing when we listen:

- *receiving* the sounds and sights from the other person's voice and body and transmitting them via our auditory and optic nerves to our brain
- *recognising* the codes (words, jargon, phraseology, similes, body language etc) used by the other person to communicate to us what is in their mind
- *integrating* the codes in two ways: first, integrating them so that the individual bits of information form a coherent message; second, integrating this message with information already in our brain enabling us, for example, to appreciate, analyse, criticise, agree, disagree etc
- *storing* the bits of information in such a way that we can recall them at will and link them with other bits of information so that they can be used for many different purposes.

Consider listening in the light of this sequence. You can listen passively – that is, without engaging the speaker in dialogue. You cannot query parts of the message, check your understanding, seek justification, and so on. *Receiving* the bits of information will not be a problem (as long as there is no interference such as noise or visual distractions). *Recognising* could be a problem if the speaker uses codes with which you are unfamiliar. For example a computer with a '686 chip' or with a speed of '66 MHz' no doubt means a lot to people who understand them; a 'permanently inoperative hostile combatant' no doubt means a lot to someone in the military; 'touching base' and 'running it up the flagpole to see if anyone salutes it' is no doubt very precise terminology to people who are familiar with those phrases. *Integrating* can be a problem if the speaker's thoughts are unstructured or if the speaker has a different frame of reference from you. *Storing* and *recalling* can be problems if the messages are unclear to you. Listening to a lecture would be a good example: if you know where the subject fits into the larger body of information and if the lecture is well structured, presented in terms you understand, and delivered in a memorable way you will have few problems listening passively. If on the other hand it is not well presented you would wish, no doubt, to listen actively.

When listening actively you engage the speaker in dialogue and use behaviours that help you listen in the full sense of the word. Table 3.1 lists behaviours that will help you appreciate the difference between active listening, passive listening and not listening at all. This last category is very important so, as you read the table, ask yourself which of these behaviours you would do well to exhibit less, and which you would do well to exhibit more.

Notice how, in Table 3.1, the signs associated with not listening that are on the bottom row of the table are obvious. Those in the middle, however, are the kinds of behaviours many people display even though they *are* listening. The important point to note is that you will look as if you are *not* listening. You may also be making it more difficult to listen well. Lengthy note-taking, for example, will be slower than the speed of the talker's speech and can cause you to miss what is coming next; doodling will mean that you are listening with your ears only and not with your eyes as well. Because the eyes are a major highway for information travelling to the brain you are limiting your ability to listen well.

Hence my emphasis on the need to listen actively. You not only look as if you are listening, you prove that you are listening by probing, summarising, and checking understanding. Listening this way has several benefits. The other person finds you satisfying to talk to because, as I said earlier, we like listeners. We also like people who appear interested in us, make an effort to understand, do not jump to conclusions, and so on. You clear up any recognition problems and find it easier to integrate and store the speaker's message. You find the listening process more satisfying because you are involved in it. Finally you are building or maintaining a relationship with the speaker in a way that passive listening cannot achieve.

Table 3.1
Listening behaviours

Signs associated with active listening	Helpful eye contact. Looking relaxed and receptive. Making encouraging sounds and gestures.	Minimal note-taking. Asking relevant questions. Making relevant comments.	Summarising. Checking understanding.
Signs associated with passive listening	Helpful eye contact. Looking relaxed and receptive.	Making encouraging sounds and gestures.	Minimal note-taking
Signs associated with not listening	Lengthy note-taking. Negative facial expressions such as frowns and scowls. Positioning yourself too close or too far away. Looking inappropriately laid back.	Being distracted. Fidgeting and doodling. Sitting or standing away from the other person. Losing eye contact. Closing your eyes. Yawning.	Clock-watching while the other person is speaking. Making hurry up gestures. Interrupting. Abruptly changing the subject.

Summary

Probing and listening are vital and complementary skills. In particular, probing is such a universal tool that most of us can easily make more and better use of it. We need to be careful however that the natural speed of our thinking does not tempt us into unproductive sorts of questions. Listening is a more complicated process than most of us realise at first. We can achieve much more by listening actively. This has nothing to do with wiggling our ears but everything to do with taking an active part in the listening process. This involves probing, summarising, checking understanding, and displaying the sort of body language that confirms we are listening. Active listening helps us integrate and store information and come across to the speaker in a positive light.

Getting on the same wavelength

Trying to influence someone who is not on the same wavelength as us is very difficult. Influencing is easier if you and the other person are 'in tune'. This section shows you how to use a variety of skills to remove unnecessary obstacles and achieve that synchronisation. In doing so it speeds up the conversation and lessens the likelihood that the other person will misinterpret what you are saying. Some aspects of it also enable you to be seen as a trustworthy person.

Why is it necessary to get on the same wavelength? We human beings have a brain that is geared up to be a kind of recognition machine. We see something, check our data banks, and know what it is. It may be a motor car emerging from a junction that we know to be dangerous; the pin-stripe-suited man with the loud tie and bright red braces who we assume works in stocks and shares; the shifty eyes of the salesman that we spot as a sign of dishonesty. Most of this 'recognition' is very useful.

Once we categorise something, however, there are two by-products:

- First, we filter all further information according to that categorisation. So the loud-mouthed drunk in the hospital we see only as a loud-mouthed drunk, and react accordingly. (The thought that he might be basically a decent man who has just been given some bad news, and drinking is his way of coping temporarily, might not even enter our heads.)
- Second, we find it very difficult to switch from one thinking pattern to another without a rather large jolt.

Anyone who has seen the well-known trick picture of the old woman which also happens to be that of a beautiful young lady will know what I mean. Even when the 'other' picture is pointed out to people they can have tremendous difficulty switching from the image they saw first.

This 'recognition' phenomenon, together with its by-products of filtering and thinking patterns, happens in conversation. The perfectly genuine question can be seen as an objection; the pointing-out of a problem can be seen as the making of an obstacle. The result is that the people in the dialogue are no longer on the

Figure 3.1

What do you see: a beautiful young woman – or an old hag?

same wavelength. Their thoughts are out of sychronisation. They are moving further apart rather than closer together.

Behaviour to help people get on the same wavelength falls into two categories: conversational behaviours, and the more formal behaviours you will find useful in a group discussion. There are five behaviours in all that help in conversational focusing.

1 Signposting

Signposting is amazingly simple and wonderfully beneficial. It clarifies the communication process by attracting the other person's attention and relieving them of the need to categorise the information they are receiving. They can devote all their attention therefore to what is being said without distracting themselves by incorrectly 'recognising' the category of message. It is also something that most people occasionally do quite naturally. Let me first define it: it is a way of letting the other person know what sort of communication you are about to send. It grabs their attention, prepares them, thus improving their receptivity, and increases the chances that they will be 'on the same wavelength'. Here are some examples:

- As soon as you begin a sentence with 'On the one hand . . .' your listener knows that you are about to give one viewpoint that will be followed quickly by a different viewpoint, '. . . but on the other hand . . .'.
- As soon as you say, 'Let me ask you a question' your listener

is ready and waiting for the question and knows that you are not about to make an objection, play devil's advocate, or whatever.

- As soon as you say, 'Here's an example' everyone knows that you are about to give an example of something you have just described and that you are not about to embark on a separate point.
- As soon as you say, 'Let me see if I understand you correctly. What I think you are saying is . . .' your listener knows you are about to check your understanding of what they are saying.
- As soon as you say, 'Let me sum up to see if we agree so far' your listener knows you are about to summarise, which will give them an opportunity to see if they agree with your summary.

These are easy, everyday examples, but signposting works in more complex situations too. I sometimes have people on courses who want to know how to broach a sensitive subject with someone. A problem of increasing frequency is where someone is promoted to run a section 'over the head' of a member of staff who thought they were the heir apparent. The member of staff then appears resentful and unco-operative towards the new manager. The manager wants to discuss the matter but is unsure how to open the conversation and is afraid that they will appear either too confrontational or too soft. Depending on the exact circumstances my advice is often this: at the end of a routine meeting with the person put down your pen, close the file, or do something to signal that that part of the discussion is over. Then say calmly, in a neutral tone of voice, 'There's something I'd like to discuss with you. It's a bit sensitive so may I just describe how it looks to me?' The member of staff will know that the conversation is about to take a different direction; that it is a sensitive matter; and that you are going to describe something from your point of view, which implies that you are going to make neither judgements nor accusations. You have also requested their permission to describe it, which signals that you respect them. It is also an easy few words to remember and practise so that they can be delivered fluently. You are therefore less likely to deliver them too abruptly or too submissively.

Signposting is simple, effective, and yet we do not do it often enough. We forget that we have maybe thought the issue through; that it makes sense to us; that we know our 'gameplan' and so on. Here is an analogy. (Incidentally, that was a signpost for you; you are now ready for an analogy.) Imagine throwing a handful of jigsaw pieces to someone every few minutes and asking them gradually to complete the jigsaw. The chances are that they would either have great difficulty or that they would give up in disgust at the impossibility of the task. On the other hand (another signpost for you) if you let them see the picture of the completed jigsaw and say to them, 'This handful is from the top right-hand corner', they might actually find the task an enjoyable challenge. *You* know where the handful of jigsaw pieces fits in; it will help them if *they* know too. Similarly in conversation you know where your words fit into the bigger picture; signposting will help the other person know where they fit in too.

A word of warning, however: do not signpost disagreement. 'I'm going to disagree with you for the following reasons . . .' will cause problems. Signposting disagreement sends the other person's brain into overdrive about why you are disagreeing, how they can counter that disagreement, what it will mean for them, and so on. They will probably not listen to your reasons, but even if they do their mind will be in an unproductive thought pattern. Far better, when you need to disagree, to give your reasons and then state that, for those reasons, you have to disagree.

2 Checking your understanding

A small difference in understanding at the start of a conversation may be imperceptible but as the conversation progresses (and especially after the two parties go to implement what they have agreed) the small difference can have grown into a major difference. If you check your understanding of the other person's point of view, concerns, intended actions, or whatever, you avoid such problems. You also come across as being interested in the other person and concerned about getting it right.

One last point: checking is most useful when done as a summary. Part-way through a conversation it forms a good way of punctuating different parts of the discussion. At the end of a conversation it is a nice way of rounding off the discussion with a final check of understanding.

3 Asking questions

As I have mentioned before, questions are the positive influencer's most versatile tool. One of the benefits is that we can use them to focus the other person's attention on issues of our choosing. The alternative is often to have a dialogue where you say something, followed by the other person saying something, followed by you saying something, and so on – a bit like verbal tennis. The other person is free to move off at tangents and avoid issues you would like to address. If on the other hand they are responding to your questions the discussion will stay focused.

4 Self-disclosure

This is the act of sharing how you feel with someone else. You are literally disclosing something about yourself, letting them know that you feel awkward, embarrassed, unsure or pleased, proud or delighted. Perhaps it is because they are being open about things that many of us are inclined to leave unsaid people who use self-disclosure come across as very open and honest.

We are usually more ready to share pleasant emotions than unpleasant ones, so the latter will be my main focus when describing self-disclosure. Sharing negative feelings and emotions is not something that we do very often, especially at work. We frequently feel that feelings and emotions are not really acceptable topics for conversation or that if we let the other person know we feel confused (for example) we will appear vulnerable. In actual fact the opposite is more likely to be true.

Telling someone 'I feel uncomfortable when you speak to me like that' or 'It concerns me that you feel that way' or 'I feel a bit anxious saying this, however . . .' brings feelings and emotions out into the open, which is good because it is only in the open that they can be resolved. Furthermore, feelings and worries are going to affect us whether we admit to them or not, so we might as well do so and make them a legitimate part of the conversation.

Doing so has several benefits. First, the other person's thoughts begin to synchronise with yours; they join you on the same 'wavelength'. They understand better what you are saying and why you are saying it. You are providing context, which helps them understand you. Second, to admit openly to a worry or anxiety is something that is usually done by only people with sound self-esteem, so you appear to be a confident person without any danger of overstepping the mark into arrogance. Third, it brings into the discussion issues of significance that we are all too inclined to leave to one side. We are all affected by what we think and feel yet because we are accustomed to keeping such things hidden, lest we are seen as weak and emotional, they are rarely put on the table for discussion.

Finally people who use self-disclosure appropriately are generally seen as open, honest and trustworthy. That can be especially relevant when praising someone. For example saying 'Well done for the way you handled that customer complaint' will not have the same impact as 'You handled that customer very effectively. It makes me pleased to see what we teach on training programmes being used so effectively. Well done.' But, as I say, self-disclosure works only if it is used appropriately. So let us look at what I mean by 'appropriately'.

Like adding spice to a meal, a little will enhance the flavour while too much will destroy it. Self-disclosure needs to be used sparingly. We need also to maintain a neutral expression and tone of voice (unless we are praising someone), make eye contact and use open gestures. An anxious expression, a whining or 'oily' voice, evasive looks away, and protective gestures will make self-disclosure counter-productive.

5 Defusing emotive language

Most of us have been in situations where emotions are running high and what we really want to do is deliver a clear and unequivocal message to someone. Unfortunately the emotional element can cause problems.

First, it can trigger our fight-or-flight response and in so doing send us down the submissive or aggressive route. On the submissive route we fear conflict and so water down our comments, which lose their impact. We then feel bad about ourselves for being a wimp. On the aggressive route we go in too hard, usually exaggerating the case and using the sort of language that makes the other person remember less of what we said and more of how we said it. Second, the emotional element can trigger the other person's fight-or-flight response, sending them down the submissive or aggressive routes. This response can happen even if we simply choose words that happen to trigger the wrong reaction. It may be unreasonable or 'over-emotional' of the other person but, remember, one of our principles is that 'pulling' at their pace is more effective than 'pushing' at ours.

What we want to avoid is the issue we wanted to address becoming lost in a fog of emotion. What we need to do therefore is select terminology that is accurate, easy for us to say, and less likely to be received emotionally by the other person. Consider the following pairs of expressions and ask yourself which is the more accurate, the easier to say, and the more 'palatable' to hear:

'You're not performing.'	'I have some concerns about your performance that I'd like to discuss with you, please.'
'You're too lazy.'	'Are you aware that you give the impression of being lazy?'
'What you ought to do is . . .'	'What would be the effect if you . . .?'
'According to your staff, you're too detached.'	'Are you aware that your staff perceive you as detached?'

If you are at all aggressive you may prefer the left-hand of the pairs, but I would suggest that if we take the first one as an example you are likely to get a defensive or counter-attacking response. Alternatively if you choose the right-hand of the pair you are likely to get a request for more details, which means that the subject has been broached and the conversation commenced.

Meetings and group discussions

So far we have looked at signposting, checking your understanding, asking questions, self-disclosure, and defusing emotive language. All these behaviours are as useful in group discussions such as meetings as they are in ordinary conversation. The problem of group discussions is however that as there are more people involved, and hence a greater variety of wavelengths for people to be on, the propensity for problems is greater.

Imagine being in a meeting where someone makes a suggestion. The suggestion may be imperfect but it has a few good points going for it. Other people in the meeting may react in different ways. One person may spot the potential in the suggestion and try to build on it. Another may spot a flaw in the suggestion and try to point out the problems. Another may focus on costs or other facts such as timescale, staff requirements, facilities needed etc. Another may not like the idea for emotional reasons, pointing out that it looks like change for the sake of it or that staff will not like the shift in values that the suggestion embraces. They are all talking about the same suggestion but they are not on the same wavelength. The result is an unsatisfactory discussion. In fact this is how many otherwise good ideas are stifled at birth.

Imagine the difference however if the chairperson (or anyone for that matter) proposed that everyone involved in the discussion proceeded in an orderly fashion. For example they could say, 'OK, Jean has just come up with a suggestion. Let's spend the next few minutes talking about it. First let's build on it, see if we can knock it into some sort of shape. Next, we'll talk facts. See how much it might cost, what staff requirements and facilities it might take. Then we'll all do some negative thinking, see what problems we can identify. Finally, we'll all talk openly, describing how we feel about the suggestion. Who'd like to go first?'

Adopting this sort of approach helps get everyone on the same wavelength. The thinking behind it is that there is nothing wrong with anyone's input to the discussion. The problem is in the lack of co-ordination and sequencing. A bit like with an orchestra someone might be playing the right notes but if they are playing them at the wrong time in the music then the whole thing sounds dreadful. This co-ordination should be the job of the chairperson but in 20 years I have never seen anyone chair a meeting this way, nor have I suggested this method to anyone without it coming as a surprise to them. Most of the surprise, I suspect, is because, having heard it, it sounds so obvious.

Whenever a discussion flounders it is worth asking yourself whether it is because people are on different wavelengths and, if so, proposing that you all co-ordinate your thinking. If someone proposes an idea the next, most productive action to take might be to develop it; if someone makes a statement that triggers people's emotions the next, most productive thing to do might be to talk openly about how everyone feels about it. To help co-ordinate the discussion it can be very worthwhile to nominate someone as the *process manager*. That person takes no part in the meeting. Their role is to observe and comment on the appropriateness of the behaviours in the discussion and the direction in which those behaviours are leading the conversation. They need to avoid becoming involved in the meeting because it is difficult to concentrate on the subject matter and the process at the same time. Their input might be to make comments such as 'We seem to be getting bogged down in costs on this one yet we haven't determined exactly what the benefits would be'; or 'John, you're pushing that one idea very forcefully but a moment ago everyone agreed that you would all generate as many alternatives as possible. Your persistent reference to the alternative you proposed is hindering the generation of other ideas'; or 'It seems as if the discussion has lost some momentum. Let me summarise the main arguments for and against and then perhaps we can take a decision.' This is the role we often expect of the chairperson but in reality they often have either too much of a stake in the outcome of the discussion or are too busy gathering information to be efficient at observing the process. Not to mention the fact that the chairperson just might happen to be the most senior person attending the meeting, which is no guarantee of ability to manage the process of the discussion itself. It is often worthwhile therefore to bring in someone to act as process manager who has no vested interest in the outcome of the discussion. (If you would like a more detailed description of getting on the same wavelength in groups I would recommend *Six Thinking Hats* (London, Penguin, 1990) by Edward de Bono.)

Summary

We know from our description of listening that it is by no means a straightforward process. We also know from our own experience that people can easily misunderstand one another or react emotionally. *We* know the context of the message into which our individual sentences fit. *We* know where the thrust of our argument is leading. Unless the other person is gifted with mental telepathy, *they* will not know these things. Your innocent question may be seen as a sign that you disagree, that you are a doubting Thomas or that you are playing devil's advocate. When people get together in groups the propensity for problems is increased as people think positively, negatively, factually, and emotionally all at different times. In any of these cases you are on different wavelengths. Far better to signpost, check understanding, use questions to focus attention, use self-disclosure, employ 'palatable' language and, in groups especially, manage the discussion process. That way you stay on the same wavelength and the task of influencing is so much easier. After all if the other person can see where you are going it is much easier for them to follow you.

Persuasive selling

As I mentioned in the introduction to this chapter if your experience of salespeople has only been of the manipulative variety you may wonder why I have included persuasive selling in a book on positive influencing skills. Put simply it is because some salespeople are non-manipulative and we can learn a lot about influencing from them. So in this section we will look at some 'facts of life' in selling, how effective salespeople respond to those facts of life, and finally what we, as positive influencers, can learn from them, and how we can use those lessons.

Facts of life

While salespeople are no doubt all keen to make a sale some realise certain 'facts of life' and take them into account when selling. The main ones are described below. You may be able to think of exceptions to them but they are probably the exceptions that prove the rule.

- *It is easier and more cost-effective to retain customers than it is to replace lost ones.* It is therefore in the interests of salespeople to keep their customers satisfied. That way their customers have neither the need nor the desire to find other suppliers.

- *Customers make purchase decisions not salespeople.* Customers need therefore to feel comfortable with the purchase decision. They also need to feel comfortable with the sales process that led to the decision.
- *Customers buy something to fulfil a need.* It is an old saying in selling that no one buys an electric drill because they want an electric drill. They buy it because they want a hole in the wall! Similarly no one buys a burglar alarm because they want a burglar alarm. They buy one because they want protection. People rarely buy a motor car because they want some metal set on four wheels; they want a means of transport. If at this stage you are also thinking, 'Yes, but they might also want what marketing people refer to as a 'lifestyle statement', then you have just hit an important nail on the head. That is, many purchase decisions are made with a mixture of rationality and emotion. Picture if you will a young executive about to buy a motor car. He knows that it has to accommodate his wife and two young children plus their toys and baby carriages, not to mention shrubs from the garden centre and weekly shopping. What he needs is a sensible estate car but what his heart is set on is a sports coupé because it fits his self-image, will impress the other sales executives where he works, will have the right impact on his friends, and so on. The need may be emotional as well as material but people still buy to fulfil the need.
- *Products and features have services but customers buy benefits.* A feature, in this instance, is a characteristic of the product or service; a benefit is what that characteristic does for the customer. A school may possess a pupil/teacher ratio of 15:1 but parents will buy the individual attention for their children and the academic advantage it brings. A computer manufacturer may offer 12 months' on-site maintenance with every new computer, but customers buy a hassle-free period. A fashion-clothes store may offer a charge card with regular monthly statements and special opening hours for charge-card customers during sales, but customers buy the security of always knowing their financial commitments, a feeling of privilege, and a chance to secure the best bargains. This feature/benefit concept can be taken quite far. According to some recent research one of the benefits that McDonald's customers buy is predictability! They know what will be on the menu, how it

will be presented, what it will taste like, and so on. Far too many salespeople forget this important distinction between features and benefits. They understand their products' features and assume that the customer will be as enthusiastic about them as they are.

- *Benefits are personal.* The same feature can deliver different benefits to different customers. A luxurious, powerful motor car (feature) might mean effortless long-distance cruising (benefit) to a customer who travels a lot, but it might mean street credibility (benefit) to a driver who spends most of their time in town traffic jams yet has ideas about self-image. A personal computer with a CD-ROM (feature) might mean easy storage and retrieval (benefit) of vast amounts of information to a financial analyst, but might mean a new world of exciting educational programs (benefit) to a parent with young children. Again, too many salespeople regard benefits as universal and assume that what is attractive to one customer will be attractive to another.

We can add to these fundamentals a few facts about people in general. On the whole we prefer talking to listening, we appreciate people who listen to us, and we receive psychological pats on the back when people pay attention to us.

How effective salespeople respond

Effective salespeople adopt an approach to selling that involves customers, finds out what is important to them, and establishes in their minds a link between what they want and what the salesperson has to offer. In doing so they create in the customer the feeling that they have been treated fairly and courteously by the salesperson, that the sales process was a rational activity leading naturally to the purchase decision and, finally, that the decision itself is a sound one. Here is a word of warning, though, which I can best illustrate with an analogy. If you were to learn, say, a martial art you could use your skills to defend yourself and other people from dangerous situations – or you could use your skills to mug people more effectively. This is a point I make when teaching assertiveness, and it applies equally to this section on persuasive selling. If your motives are one-sided you can use persuasive selling to manipulate people more effectively; if your

63

motives are genuine, as I hope they are, you can use the tactics to benefit both you and other people.

So what are these tactics that salespeople use to persuade rather than manipulate? They are based on behavioural research into both selling and negotiating as well as on a few well-known but easily forgotten fundamentals about selling. That approach is based on probing and listening – and doing so in a set sequence (described below). It might help you to appreciate the sequence better if you think of it as a target, in which you begin at the outer ring and work your way gradually towards the bull's-eye, or alternatively as a funnel in which you start at the broad opening and work your way gradually to the narrower opening.

Figure 3.2
Persuasive selling sequence

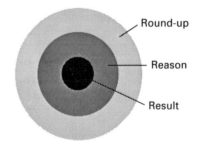

The sequence begins with the salesperson collecting information about the customer and the customer's situation. It is a 'rounding-up' exercise. Some of the information collected may be irrelevant to the sale (or may even show that the customer has no need of the product or service on offer) but some may point to the customer's need and so lead both you and the customer towards a 'reason' for the purchase which the salesperson can pursue. Because customers buy benefits, however, the salesperson will have to probe further towards exactly what the results of the purchase will be, so enabling the customer to visualise the full benefit of what the product or service will do for them – the 'result' that the customer will buy.

Here are two examples to illustrate the sequence. In the first the sequence is ignored and in the second it is used. The situation is the same for both of them. A salesperson is trying to sell a computer system to the finance director of a small company. (The salesperson speaks first.)

– Thank you for agreeing to see me, Mr Smith.
– That's OK. But if we could make it brief I'd be grateful. I'm trying to sort out customer queries on invoices.
– I just want to tell you about our new computer. I see from our records that you use a Mark One. The Mark Two has just come out. It's a much better machine and I'd like to tell you about it.
– I don't want to buy a new computer.
– But this one's much better than your existing model. It has the latest chip and a memory measured in gigabytes.
– I've got enough trouble with my current computer.
– This one comes with a free one-year on-site maintenance agreement.
– It sounds a super machine but I'm really not interested in buying one.
– You don't have to buy one, Mr Smith: our finance division will be happy to talk to you about leasing.
– I want no more financial commitments right now, thank you. Try me again in 12 months' time. Perhaps we'll be in a better position then.

This salesperson did not get very far. Too much of the conversation focused on the computer's features and there was no attempt to identify a need that the customer wanted to fulfil. Furthermore the customer was not really involved in the conversation. Let's compare it with the second example. (Again, the salesperson speaks first.)

– Thank you for agreeing to see me, Mr Smith.
– That's OK. But if we could make it brief I'd be grateful. I'm trying to sort out customer queries on invoices.
– I'll be quick then. I'm selling a new computer.
– Before you go any further, I ought to tell you that I'm not interested in buying a new computer.
– That's OK. May I ask what sort of computer you currently use?
– A Mark One.

– What do you use it for?

– Accounting, sales and purchase ledgers, invoicing, tax calculations. The usual things.

– And what do you think of it?

– Not much. It's slow, unreliable, and requires too much manual intervention for my liking.

– What kind of problems does that cause?

– Month ends are always difficult. We often have to employ contract staff to help get invoices out in time. They don't know the customers so sometimes the invoices go out incorrectly. We're a small family company and pride ourselves on personal attention but often something that's agreed over the phone then gets passed to a contract person who doesn't know the case, and before we know where we are we've upset a customer. That's why I handle all the queries personally. It's the only way to let customers know that we value them. And I can tell you in the current economic climate that's no joke. I have a personal target from the managing director to do something about the level of customer complaints.

– Why do you persevere with that computer if it isn't efficient?

– Cost. There's a recession on, you know. We don't have big reserves and I'm not into borrowing from the bank, not at today's interest rates.

– Let me make sure I understand what you've told me. You have a Mark One but you're not happy with its performance. You feel it's slow and you have to intervene manually too much. It's also causing you to spend money on contract staff. You'd consider replacing it if it weren't for the cost. But what really concerns you is the customer dissatisfaction caused by the persistent errors.

– Yes, I'd say you've understood me very well.

– Good. Now, tell me, if I could show you how to save money on contract staff, keep customers happy and, perhaps, free up some of your time – all without spending any money – would you be interested?

– Are you giving these computers away, then?

– No. However, what would be the effect on your need for contract staff if you had a reliable computer that would not only record individual customer instructions but would process everything twice as fast as is currently done?

– I wouldn't need the contract staff every month.
– And that would save you money?
– Of course.
– And if some of that money paid the lease rental on a Mark Two, would that have any negative effect on your company's cash flow?
– No, because I'd be saving on the contract staff.
– So may I tell you how the Mark Two can do all that for you?
– Please do!

This salesperson got much further than the first because he focused not on what he wanted to sell but on what Mr Smith wanted to buy – and it was not a computer! He uncovered a range of problems during the 'round-up' phase, such as the current computer's slowness and its unreliability, the need for contract staff, the problems with customers, the pride the company has in the personal attention it gives to customers, and the finance director's attitude towards money. The use of contract staff emerged as the central problem or 'reason' and the 'result' that the finance director was prepared to 'buy' was the customer satisfaction that the renewed personal service would bring. The new computer was simply the means to that end.

This approach does work. Here is a personal story. Many years ago I decided to buy a burglar alarm for my home and had several burglar alarm salespeople come to visit me over a period of days. Two of them told me how fantastic their burglar alarms were, how sensitive the detectors were, and how many decibels the alarm registered. The third salesperson told me very little to begin with. Instead he said, 'I'd like to divide our conversation into three parts. I'd like to have a look at your house to make sure I can specify the right configuration for your needs. I'd also like to tell you about our alarms because we believe they are very good ones. But first, I'd like to ask you why you want a burglar alarm?' After I had answered that question he had another, and another, and another. The questions, I am sure, were intended to provide him with the information he needed to sell to me. By the time we had finished however I was convinced of something: I did not want to buy a burglar alarm. What I wanted to buy was peace of mind! The meeting ended with my insisting on movement detectors in rooms in which he thought it was unnecessary to have them, even though it increased the cost (and his commission) compared with what he believed was necessary.

He had not tried to sell me anything in the traditional sense of the word but the process of his asking me questions caused me to crystallise my thoughts and identify the 'result' I wanted – despite his protests. I was also happy to recommend him to friends and neighbours because he was not a 'pushy' salesman. The first two salespeople had tried on the other hand to sell to me in the traditional sense of the word. I was on the receiving end of their 'sales pitch'. I was uninvolved and kept my defences high.

Review

Let us pause here and review what we have covered so far. Professional salespeople can adopt one of two routes. They can be manipulative or persuasive. The manipulative variety tries to sell you their product by putting you on the receiving end of a sales pitch. You feel passive in the sales process, occasionally trapped or tricked, and often uncomfortable. Persuasive salespeople try equally hard to make the sale but because they understand certain facts of life about selling they want you to be happy with both the purchase decision and the sales process itself. So they involve you, make genuine attempts to find out about your situation and your needs, and work at a pace that enables you to see the connection between what you need and what they are selling. They involve you in the sales process and, in so doing, help you make the purchase decision rather than have it thrust upon you.

The two extremes are easy to recognise but as usual the vast majority of people fall somewhere in the middle. So if you are unsure which type of salesperson is selling to you here are two useful tests you can apply. First, ask yourself who is doing most of the talking. If it is the salesperson, you are on the receiving end of a sales pitch. Remember that the salesperson cannot find out about you, your situation, and what you need without listening to you. Compare examples one and two that you have just read; look at the ratio of talking between salesperson and customer. The difference is dramatic. Second, ask yourself whether the salesperson is asking predominantly closed or open questions. If most of the questions are closed, beware. Closed questions are used to check information, not to gather it. Manipulative sales-people will use them to 'paint you into a corner'. They will ask you questions according to a pre-set script. Your answer to one question will determine their next question and the only 'logical' outcome will be for you to buy what they are selling. A dominance of open questions, on the other hand, implies no preconceived manipulative plan on the part of the salesperson.

What we can learn

If you go back over this section and replace the word 'customers' with 'staff', 'colleagues', 'team members' or whoever it is that you have to influence you will see why elements of persuasive selling are relevant to positive influencing. If you want someone to 'buy into' your way of thinking and sustain the relationship into the future they need to feel comfortable with both the decision and the process by which the decision was reached. They will do that if they feel involved in the process, if they feel that you have made an effort to understand them – that you have not tried to trap them, 'out-logic' them or in some other way manipulate them.

In short, while we may not want to employ these tactics in exactly the same way as salespeople we can learn from them and use their tactics to help us 'pull' rather than 'push', to involve the other person, to seek to understand, and to avoid manipulation. Here are two examples. As before, the first example shows how an attempt to influence can go wrong if the persuasive influencing tactics are not used; and the second shows how it can go right if the tactics are used. The situation concerns a training manager trying to persuade a research manager to invest time, money and effort in establishing Personal Development Plans (PDPs) for all his professional staff. The company is commercial and research is one of the sales divisions. Here is example one. (The training manager speaks first.)

– Thank you for seeing me, John. As you know, I'm keen to get PDPs into all divisions by the end of the year.
– That's as may be, but I'm taking on no new initiatives at the moment.
– I'd think carefully. Personal development is a major issue in

the company at the moment, you know.

– I know that and I'm not saying I *won't* do it. I'm just saying that, at the moment, I've got enough on my plate trying to stay competitive. There are quite a few university sales teams out there trying to pinch my customers – and in some cases being successful.

– But, surely, keeping skills up to date is important to you?

– Of course it is, but, as I said, keeping customers is even more important.

– But how will your staff feel if they see other divisions implementing PDPs while you're not?

– And how will they feel if they get made redundant because of falling revenue? I think they'd rather have a job than a PDP, don't you?

– That's not a long term view, though, is it John?

– I can drain the swamp when I've shot the crocodiles. In the meantime, I can't do anything about PDPs. Maybe next year.

Example two follows. (Again, the training manager speaks first.)

– Thank you for seeing me, John. As you know, I want to discuss PDPs with you but you mentioned over the phone that you had other priorities at the moment. So, to ensure that I understand, can we talk about the research division in general?

– OK. What do you want to know?

– Why don't we start with those other priorities? What takes up most of your time at the moment?

– That's an easy one: trying to fend off the competition.

– How is the competition changing?

– It's getting tougher. Universities are having so much funding cut that they are becoming quite aggressive in sales to make up revenue. As they still receive some state funding, however, they can generally undercut us.

– How are you and your team responding to that?

– We stress our experience compared with that of universities. Our people tend to have more industrial experience.

– How does that make a difference?

– Our people are more likely to spot problems early on in a project. They can also identify short cuts. That can save time and money.

– In what way will things change in the future?

– I think we'll lose more of the bread-and-butter contracts. We can't really compete on cost. That means going for the high-value projects.

– And what is the best way of competing for those?

– We have to ensure that we get the right experience, stay at the cutting edge of technology and that we present our knowledge, skills and experience in such a way that we stand head and shoulders above the competition.

– So you need to present the knowledge, skills and experience of your staff as a competitive advantage?

– Exactly.

– And what are you doing to ensure that their knowledge, skills and experience develops the way you want it to go to give you that competitive advantage in the future?

– Well . . . just relying on people learning from their jobs I suppose . . . and doing the right postgraduate qualifications . . . going on the right courses. That sort of thing.

– Are people getting the right experience?

– I'm not sure anyone can say that they're getting exactly the right experience.

– How do you present it to customers?

– In a kind of CV for each staff member who would be working on a contract.

– How do customers react to the CVs?

– We do need to present them better. I'm aware of that.

– And what's the staff situation like?

– At the moment it's OK but we've just done appraisals and I know that if we don't help people manage their careers better then there will be problems in the future.

– It sounds as if you need a way of managing people's careers, experience, qualifications and training so that they are fully satisfied and customers are impressed enough to give you the high-value contracts.

– You've got a magic wand, have you?

– No, just a suggestion. What you're describing is exactly what PDPs are designed to achieve.

– You'll have to explain that to me.

– I'd be glad to. Let's start with your business needs . . .

Exactly as with the salespeople the first example shows no desire to see what the research manager might need; it promotes only what the training manager wants to sell. Consequently the research manager finds it easy to resist. In the second example, the research manager has nothing to resist because all the training manager is doing is to ask him questions about his priorities; because those questions are open rather than closed there is no hint of manipulation. The training manager is however 'rounding up' vital information. He is spotting a 'reason' for the research manager to 'buy in to' his way of thinking, and also the benefits, or the 'results', that the research manager will 'buy'. Furthermore, at no time does he come across as 'pushy': the ratio of talking is well within the research manager's favour and there is no dominance of closed questions either.

So what can be learnt is that if we want to influence someone we have a simple choice. We can manipulate them, or we can adopt persuasive selling tactics. The former approach will probably result in resentment even if we succeed in getting the other person to do what we want. The latter approach gives us a better chance of successfully influencing the other person and of genuinely 'converting' them, and that conversion is therefore likely to be sustained into the future. If we want to use the persuasive selling approach, we have to remember that:

- It is the other person who has to make the decision, not us (after all, we want them to buy into our way of thinking, not vice versa).
- People 'buy' things to fulfil needs.
- What we are offering has features and benefits; the features are characteristics of the offer while the benefits are what those characteristics will do for the other person.
- If we probe and listen we may be able to round up enough information to spot reasons why the other person should agree with us and we can then present our offer in terms of the results they will receive. In doing so the process is likely to be more satisfying to the other person than if we tried to persuade them in the traditonal sense.

Using these lessons

There are four points I want to make about using these lessons. The first is that it is not easy sitting there asking questions when you know that the only logical course of action is for the other person to agree to do what you want. The answer can be as plain as a pikestaff to anyone with even a modicum of common sense. If you find yourself thinking such thoughts, remind yourself of something. Think of the last time you went to buy something, really took a dislike to the salesperson, and walked out – even though the product or service on offer was the best for you. You acted emotionally; you acted irrationally; but so what? It is *your* money! The sales process has to proceed in a way that customers are happy with. Influencing situations have to proceed in such a way that the person who is being asked to accept something is happy with it. Notice how in the second computer sales example the salesperson even proposed his solution in the form of a question so that he always moved at the finance director's pace.

The second point is that you have to progress through the sequence. If you get stuck in the 'round-up' phase the other person will become confused and wonder where the conversation is going. It is quite common therefore to probe various issues moving from 'round-up' to 'reason' and back again, but all the time you are gradually moving towards the centre of the target.

The third point is that the 'round-up' and 'reason' phases may fail to uncover anything of value! The computer salesman may find that another finance director just does not need his products and the training manager may find that the research department is not yet ready culturally to make a decent job of Personal Development Plans. Both may still try to 'close the sale' but their chances of success are minimal. Even if they do succeed their customers' satisfaction levels will quickly diminish and the relationship will not be sustained.

The fourth point is that, like all tools, persuasive selling needs to be used in appropriate situations. If your are delegating a routine task to a member of staff a quick 'Will you do this, please?' might be all that is required. If the other person really has no choice in the matter why pretend that they have? Save it for situations where you need to persuade someone to accept your way

73

of thinking, where they can turn you down if they want to, and where their commitment is essential to long-term success.

Review and preview

That concludes the first part of this section on persuasive selling. We have looked at the 'facts of life' in selling, examined how non-manipulative salespeople respond to them, and how we can learn from what those salespeople do. As well as probing and listening in a set sequence, however, those salespeople also display some behaviours regularly while avoiding others as much as possible. That is what we will look at now.

There are some behaviours that make you more persuasive and some behaviours that, while we often think of them as persuasive, do more harm than good. Some pioneering research in this area was conducted by Neil Rackham and John Carlisle in the mid 1970s, and I can heartily recommend their articles of the time, if you want more detail. A list of the main productive behaviours follows. You will notice that even though the usefulness of these behaviours was confirmed by research we have come across most of them already. The unproductive ones are covered at the end of this section under the heading 'No-noes'.

Seeking information

Successful influencers spend more time seeking information than giving it. They probe, mostly using open questions, and listen to the answers. As I mentioned in the section on probing (see pages 38–48) this gives them control of the pace and direction of the conversation, gives them thinking time, encourages the other person to think things through, and so on. As I mentioned in this section, it gives the other person a feeling of satisfaction with the process as a whole.

Testing your own understanding

Successful influencers summarise and check their understanding frequently. This helps keep people on the same wavelength and ensures that they move at the same pace. Summarising also shows that you are genuinely trying to understand. It can also form a convenient 'punctuation' between one part of a conversation and another.

Self-disclosure

They let the other person know what they are thinking and how they feel. This aids clarity and understanding and also helps them come across as very open and honest.

Signposting

They give advance warning of the type of communication they are about to transmit, so attracting attention to what they are about to say and minimising the chance of misunderstanding.

Hypothetical questions

This behaviour is very effective for a number of reasons. First, it enables you to test reaction to proposals and suggestions without actually making them. For example you could say, 'What would be your reaction if I said I wanted to . . .?' or 'How would you feel if I suggested . . .?' Second, it encourages the other person to visualise, and so appreciate, the full extent of your suggestions; for example, 'What would be the effect on your need for contract staff if you had a faster and more reliable computer?' or 'What would be the effect on staff morale if they each had a plan showing how their professional skills would be developed over, say, the next two years?' Finally, hypothetical questions enable you to bargain more effectively because you make all your proposals conditional upon the other person agreeing to something, as in 'If I agree to this, will you agree to that?' or 'I could only consider an extra discount if you were to increase the quantity you wanted to buy.'

Solution-oriented

The last point is that effective influencers are solution- rather than problem-oriented. They focus on how to rectify a situation rather than one why it went wrong. They concentrate on how to put something right rather than on who is to blame for it going wrong. This way they steer clear of the recriminations that serve only to harden attitudes and entrench positions. They encourage other people to join in the solution process.

Summary

In this section we have learnt from professional influencers – salespeople and negotiators – and I hope, established that the manipulative route might deliver a short-term result but not a long-term one. That only happens when the other person is happy with the decision we have persuaded them to make as well as the process leading to that decision. So we need to round up information, to identify a reason why the other person should agree to our proposal, and enable them to see the resultant benefit to them. We also need to practise certain behaviours: gathering information; checking your own understanding; self-disclosure; signposting; hypothetical questions; and being solution-oriented. These all help to make us better at influencing. Above all, we should remember that if we need someone else's commitment to a proposal in order for it to be successful it is *they* who need to see the logic in our case – we already see it; it is *they* and not we who make the decision whether or not to 'buy into' it. All we can do is learn from the best and put those lessons into effect.

Awareness of body language

Body language is the phrase used to describe the thousands of messages we transmit with our bodies rather than with our words. For this reason it is also referred to as non-verbal communication. Its relevance to influencing skills is that slight changes in body language can either enhance or detract significantly from our ability to influence someone else. It is essential therefore that everyone understands what the 'enhancers' and 'detractors' are. In this section we will therefore examine important dos and don'ts in the main body-language categories. To begin with, however, here are a few general points.

First, many people are intrigued, and some are mystified, by the concept of body language. They wonder how it is possible to tell so much from such small and seemingly innocent gestures. Let us take an example. When someone is lying, and they are afraid they may have been found out, their anxiety level increases. According to some specialists there is also a muscular reaction in the neck that the liar relieves by pulling his or her collar. So a trained police or customs interviewer, for instance, will look for persistent 'collar pulls' in response to certain questions. But of course some people who pull their collars in less stressful situations are just plain itchy. Very few of us need the detailed body language training that is required in certain professions. Most of us can be content with the fact that because body language was the first language we learnt we already know sufficient about it.

This statement may sound difficult to accept if you have been led to believe that body language is a mysterious subject full of intricate detail. But ask yourself how you would know whether someone was happy, sad, anxious, confident, feeling uncomfortable with your proposal, or openly concerned that more details have still to be finalised. Think about it, and you will describe a range of non-verbal signals. You will probably begin with obvious ones such as a smile or droopy eyes, a worried expression and a frown, a shift in posture or direct eye contact. The more you think about it however the more you will start to describe subtle non-verbal signals such as evasive eyes, a tightening of the lips, hand washing or using an arm to 'protect' the stomach. In real situations you will even find that you will spot and correctly interpret signals of which you were not even consciously aware. You will avoid committing yourself to a purchase because of 'something about the salesman's eyes'; you will meet someone for the first time and instantly like them without being able to state why other than to say it was 'just something about them'; you will deliver an important presentation to senior managers and know it was well received, saying, 'I can feel it in my bones'.

I once saw a clever illustration of our ability to see 'non-verbals' without realising we have in fact seen them. A group of people on a course were given two photographs. They were portrait shots of two young ladies in their early twenties. The photographs were presented as those of identical twins, and the group was asked to decide which twin they thought the more attractive. Even though the decision was unanimous none of the group could actually say why they thought this twin more attractive than the other. Only then did the course leader admit that both pictures were of the same young lady. All he had done, before duplicating the pictures, was slightly to enlarge the pupils of one of the 'twins'. She was the one everyone agreed was the more attractive (even though they could not say why). In other words they had seen and interpreted the larger pupils without realising they had done so. That is how observant we are about body language even when we do not realise it.

We do not need to learn the minute intricacies of body language to be better at influencing. All we need to do is raise our awareness about the subject in terms of both the signals we transmit and of the signals we receive from others.

A second general point about body language is that subtle, individual gestures are with a few exceptions rarely important. What is important are *clusters* of behaviours and the *timing* of changes. The former are important because in a cluster there are lots of gestures all transmitting and therefore confirming the same message. The latter are important because they usually occur in response to an inner reaction of some sort.

Here is an example. Imagine you are conducting a selection interview. As the candidate is telling you about how he successfully structured a section of his organisation he leans back in his chair, is inclined to one side, gesticulates naturally with one hand while the elbow of the other rests on the arm of the chair, his legs are crossed openly (the ankle of one leg resting on the knee of the other), his mouth is in a permanent smile while he talks, and his voice is firm and clear. Judging by this cluster of behaviour, how would you say he feels? Most people would say very relaxed and confident. Imagine that you then ask him a question that probes rather incisively into his role in this restructuring. He still leans back in his chair but sits more upright, he clasps both hands together, one arm still resting on that of the chair but the other now pulled tightly across his stomach, his legs change from an open cross to a closed one (the back of one knee resting on top of the other knee), his smile begins to flicker, and his voice becomes more hesistant as he stumbles for the words to answer. Judging by this new cluster of behaviour, how would you say he feels now? Most people would say distinctly nervous. And what would you say about the timing of the change? Your question about his role in the restructuring must have touched a nerve, and if his experience in structurings is material to the assessment process then the matter should be probed in more detail.

A third point is that because we do not think very much about our body language it tends to come out unedited. So by looking at clusters and changes you can tell a lot about what is going on in someone's mind even if they are trying to give a different impression.

Fourth, by looking at clusters and changes other people can tell a lot about what is going on in your mind. When our body language supports the message we are transmitting with our words our message is credible. When it contradicts our spoken message our body language takes precedence and the spoken message lacks credibility.

The final point I would like to make is that certain aspects of body language are universally recognised. A smile is the best example. It is recognised in every culture. Many aspects of body language do not however translate from one culture to another. If you stand directly facing someone with your arms folded across your chest while making direct eye contact with them you are exhibiting, you will probably agree, a sign of challenge or even aggression. In Vietnam however that stance would be a sign of respect. If someone avoids eye contact with you then you may feel that they are being either evasive or very submissive. In Japan however they may just be showing deference to you. And if you want real confusion, try disagreeing with someone from southern India by shaking your head. They will be delighted that you have just agreed with them! What follows therefore applies mostly to North Europeans and North Americans.

So most of us already know enough about the subject – even the subtleties. All we have to do is increase our awareness of clusters of body language and the timing of body-language changes – our own as well as other people's. The focus of the information below is on influencing: the non-verbal signals that will make it easier for you to influence someone else, and those that will make it more difficult. We will look at each body-language area in turn (but please bear in mind that clusters of signals are more important than individual ones) and then look at how individual signals can form clusters sending important messages.

Eyes

The eyes can transmit a variety of messages. Looking directly at someone can signal interest, confidence, or aggression. Looking away from someone can signal lack of interest, dismissiveness, lack of confidence, or submissiveness. There are subtleties as well. Our pupils dilate when we look at something that gives us pleasure. In Britain we tend to use our eyes to signal to another person that we are ending our contribution to a conversation and it is now their turn to speak. The salient aspect of our eyes lies however in looking at or looking away from someone else.

When we are listening at a normal social distance for example we tend to look at the speaker's face and concentrate our gaze within a triangle from eyebrows to mouth. When we are talking comfortably and confidently in a normal social interaction we tend to look at the same triangle. When we wish to make a serious point, however, and are confident in making it we shift our gaze to a smaller triangle from the eyes to the middle of the forehead. When we are nervous, emotionally uncomfortable, or submissive we often avert our eyes downwards and away from the other person. It is worth considering the reason for this habit.

According to research, parents make the most persistent eye contact with their children when they are reprimanding or criticising them. To a child this is both uncomfortable and threatening and the quickest relief is to avert one's eyes downwards to signify subservience. Because even the offspring of kind, loving parents gets reprimanded and criticised persistent eye contact is something many of us learn to find uncomfortable. We also learn the corresponding response of averting our eyes and carry this habit into adulthood, applying it to any situation that makes us feel emotionally uncomfortable. So as well as averting our eyes when, say, the boss reprimands us we also avert our eyes when disagreeing with someone, making a request, or standing up for ourselves.

The effect of this eye aversion is to undermine our case. If you have difficulty with eye contact try looking within the eye/mouth triangle and then, when finishing your sentence, shifting your gaze to the eye/forehead triangle. The other person will not know that you are not looking them in the eye. They will know just that you are serious. It is however worth avoiding total and persistent eye contact, especially when talking to a submissive person, because it can be intimidating. Eye contact between 50 and 70 per cent of the time is enough to make people feel that you are attentive. And if you always accompany a serious point with eye contact you will stand a much better chance of being taken seriously.

Similarly when watching someone else your can tell how confident they feel by the amount of eye contact they make with you. If it is minimal and they avert their eyes downwards you can assume they lack confidence in what they are saying (which is not the same as a lack of conviction, by the way). Alternatively if they pierce you with sustained eye contact they may be subduing anger or they may be trying to intimidate you.

Tone of voice

Tone of voice is as important as eye contact. People infer a lot from tone of voice without necessarily realising it. To avoid over-complication it will help if you think of tone of voice as being made up of the emphasis we place on different words, the pitch of the sound, the volume of our speech, and its speed. When we are cool, calm and collected all the ingredients are moderate. The emphasis we place on various words serves to help the communication process. It is usually on factual words rather than personal or emotive ones. Our pitch is comfortable. We speak neither too loudly nor too softly and our speed of speech has just the right pace in it. When we become angry, however, all that changes. We emphasise emotive words, the pitch of our voice (usually) goes lower, while volume and pace increase. When we are feeling nervous our voice becomes quieter, pitch and speed often increase and we emphasise conciliatory, apologetic and sympathy-seeking words. We also tend to ramble, speaking far more than we need to, as if we know that conflict may arise when we finish speaking and so we try to put it off as long as possible by going on and on. To display confidence in your case therefore you need a neutral tone of voice.

Emphasis has to go on factual words, and pitch, volume and speed all have to be relatively neutral. Posture helps greatly with tone of voice so that is what we will look at next.

Posture

I will divide information on posture into two, dealing first with how posture affects voice and then looking at the sorts of posture that help or hinder when influencing. First, your voice. In order for you to speak, air must pass through the vocal chords – two ribbons of muscle located in the larynx or 'Adam's apple'. The sound produced as air passes through the vocal chords then resonates in the mouth and nasal passages. In so doing it is altered according to the shape of the mouth and position of the tongue. The start of the process is however air passing through the vocal chords. The air comes from the lungs and is drawn into and exhaled from the lungs owing to the movement of the diaphragm – a large flat muscle separating the chest area from the abdominal cavity. Without the correct posture the diaphragm has insufficient room to move up and down and so cause air to be drawn into the lungs and then exhaled through the vocal chords. The equation is therefore a simple one: poor posture equals poor voice and good posture equals good voice. So what kind of posture leads to a poor or a good voice? – Exactly those that hinder or help influencing.

Posture can signify a lot about the way we feel. When feeling vulnerable we tend to 'close up' just as if we were protecting ourselves physically. The main part of our body that we protect is the abdomen. A typical action might be to fold our arms tightly across the stomach or to put one arm across the stomach in a quasi-relaxed posture. Many people do of course sit with their arms folded or with an arm across their bodies quite comfortably and signify nothing by it; so remember that we are looking for *clusters* of behaviour and part of the cluster we would look for is the tightness of the arms across the stomach, and their height. In a closed, protective posture they tend to be lower than in a relaxed posture. We also tend when feeling vulnerable to cross our legs knee to knee rather than ankle to knee. In an attempt to make ourselves appear smaller we 'shrink' a little, lowering the shoulders and curling the torso.

When feeling aggressive we do the opposite and attempt to appear bigger. Whether standing or sitting we stretch up with our backs and puff out our chests (sometimes exaggerating the size of our chests by folding our arms high across them). We also tend to hold ourselves relatively rigid, which means that, once puffed out, the chest tends to stay that way, interfering with inhaiation and exhalation.

The effect of both postures is to give the diaphragm too little room to move and the lungs insufficient space to expand. In the closed posture the diaphragm is squashed up against the digestive system and the lung cavity is contracted. In the expansive one we tend to hold our chests in a puffed-up position that interferes with breathing. The most comfortable and efficient breathing occurs when the diaphragm has room to move down (you should be able to see your abdomen rise and fall as you breathe) and the lungs have room to expand and contract. Whether standing or sitting, that means a relatively upright posture and above all a relaxed one. This posture not only makes you look more relaxed but makes you *feel* more relaxed. This may have something to do with the fact that regular and efficient breathing is a feature of all meditation and relaxation techniques.

Something else we can do with our posture to appear (and feel) more relaxed is to sit or stand *asymmetrically*. If you imagine a vertical dotted line down someone's middle, and they are symmetrical either side of that line, they probably look ill at ease, serious, formal, or aggressive. Think of a television newsreader. They sit symmetrically, directly facing the camera. It is appropriate to the serious and formal nature of their message. Compare their posture with that of a television interviewer interviewing a politician in a one-to-one 'breakfast' programme. They sit asymmetrically. Think of a nervous person attending a panel interview. They are probably sitting symmetrically but as (one hopes) they relax their posture shifts to become more asymmetrical. Another feature of a relaxed or informal posture is that, whether sitting or standing, we rarely adopt a 'full frontal' position. That is, we do not point all our body at the other person. We may point our head at them and even the upper part of our torso but our hips, legs and feet are probably pointing away from them. A full frontal position often signifies formality, confrontation, and (even) aggression.

Think of two extremes: a counselling conversation and a formal disciplinary interview. In the counselling conversation you will achieve more if you sit in a relaxed, asymmetrical posture with the bottom half of your body pointing slightly away from the person you are counselling. In the disciplinary interview you will set a more formal tone if you sit in a symmetrical posture directly opposite the other person.

In considering what type of posture is best for influencing you need to consider what type of influencing situation you are in. Is it formal or informal? In most situations it will look better if you stick more to the informal, partly because you will look more relaxed and hence confident in your position, and partly because it is more likely to be appropriate. Unless an influencing situation is very serious or highly procedural, looking confidently relaxed will add to your credibility. It tends to be people unsure of their position or nervous of their ability who need the 'security blanket' of formality when it is not relevant. In seeking the support of unncessary formality they undermine their own credibility.

A final point on posture concerns **mirroring**. When two people in conversation are in agreement they tend to 'mirror' each other's posture. Whether standing at a bar or sitting around a coffee-table, whether discussing football, politics, or the organisation's five-year plan, if they are in agreement they will tend to mirror each other's posture. They will break away from mirroring when an issue arises about which they disagree.

Proximity

Proximity is often related to posture so will look at that next. To assist understanding, here is a general point about proximity that provides the context for the points of particular relevance to influencing. We tend to be comfortable with a certain amount of space around us and we feel uncomfortable if someone else 'invades' it. The amount of space we feel is ours depends on two things: first, the situation we are in, and second, what we are used to.

As for situation we each have several 'zones' around us. The farthest away is the *public zone*. It is about 3.5 metres away from us and it is the distance we like to be from a large group of people we are addressing. Closer than that, in such a situation, and we feel uncomfortable. Next comes the *social zone*, extending from about 1 to 3.5 metres from us. This is the distance we like to keep people we do not know very well, such as the gas repairman, a shop assistant, a new employee, and so on. Next comes the *personal zone*, which extends from about 50 centimetres to 1 metre. This is the distance at which we feel comfortable at social and friendly gatherings. Next comes the *intimate zone*, which extends from 15 to 50 centimetres. It is by far the most important to us. We guard it closely and feel very uncomfortable or even threatened if someone unwelcome enters it. It is usually reserved for lovers, parents, spouse, children, and very close friends and relatives. From 0 to 15 centimetres there is a *close intimate zone* which can only really be entered during physical contact. Watch two lovers kissing and you will see that they are well within this zone from head to toe. Then watch two friends kiss, say after a dinner party, and they will deliberately keep their pelvic regions about 15 centimetres apart.

What we are used to plays a part within these overall guidelines. Someone brought up in a crowded city will feel comfortable with smaller zones than someone brought up in a sparsely populated rural area.

While the concept of zones does not apply in some situations, such as on crowded public transport, if we are to be comfortable with other people and they with us we need to stay within the appropriate zone. If you are too far away for a given set of circumstances you will appear ill at ease; if you are too close you will make the other person nervous. I have seen people giving sales presentations or presentations to senior managers fail to establish the right rapport with their audience because they have tried to get too close. I have seen interviewers make interviewees feel nervous because they have placed their chair in the public rather than the social zone. I have seen people who, when welcoming new employees, have tried to be friendly and put an arm around their shoulder – only to make them feel uncomfortable. I have unfortunately also seen people try to manipulate someone else by invading their space, adopting an aggressive posture and making excessive eye contact.

Gestures

As with other aspects of body language it is possible to send positive and negative signals with your gestures, and also to assess how someone else is receiving you by the gestures they make. So here we will look at the main categories of gestures.

- We show anxiety in relation to another person by protecting ourselves with, say, folded arms but often we hug or hang onto our arms at the same time. We can achieve the same feeling of security by leaving one arm dangling by our side but bringing the other one across it hold it or by hugging a file or a bag close to our chest. Even clasping our hands in front of our groin can make us feel slightly more secure in an anxiety-producing situation. It is a favourite gesture of people who are about to be introduced to a group of other people.
- Anxiety, especially when we feel threatened, causes our palms to produce sweat which we remove by 'washing' them together.
- Anger and aggression cause us to 'attack' the other person with our forefinger either by shaking it at them or by jabbing it in their direction. This is a favourite gesture of parents and schoolteachers when reprimanding children. Unfortunately it is also a gesture that some people adopt with other adults when stressing a point. Children do not like it and neither do adults, whatever the motives of the offending person.
- Sometimes, when we disagree with something, we erect a physical barrier by folding our arms between us and the other person. It would probably be accompanied by a slight backwards and upwards movement of the head.
- When we are listening to someone and considering what they are saying we often put a hand up to our cheek or our chin. The hand in no way supports our head, however, as that is an obvious sign of boredom.
- When we wish to indicate sincerity we frequently show people the palms of our hands. (If you are not sure about this one, stand in front of a mirror and 'sell' yourself a second-hand car, saying, 'And it's only had one careful lady owner.' Unfortunately this is a gesture overused by everyone from politicians to second-hand car salespeople when trying to convince us of something. But in everyday situations you should be safe with this gesture, if used sparingly.
- When we disapprove of something but feel constrained about

saying so, we often exhibit displacement activity such as turning our face away from the speaker and picking imaginary lint from our clothes. A speaker who is not tuned into body language would pass over this signal, but one who is alert would invite the lint-picker to share their thoughts.

• When we are talking to someone and feel both superior and confident we often 'steeple' our fingers. It is a gesture common amongst managers and professionals such as accountants and lawyers when giving advice to clients or staff.

These are the main gestures of which I want you to be aware. There are many, many others. Having looked at aspects of body language such as eyes, tone of voice, posture, proximity, and gestures let us pull the various threads together by looking at some examples of clusters and timing.

Example 1

Jack is working on a project with Bill, someone of equal status from another department. The company is beginning to utilise project teams more and more but still retains many aspects of the old hierarchical approach to management. Both Jack and Bill are under pressure of work. Jack, recognising the importance of the project, has delegated much of his routine work to a member of staff. Bill has taken the opposite approach and has delegated significant elements of the project to a member of his staff. Jack believes that without Bill's experience and personal attention the project will flounder. He is in Bill's office, speaking to him about the project. They sit either side of Bill's desk. Jack raises the subject of Bill's decision and begins to describe why he thinks the project will suffer. At the start of Jack's explanation Bill sits facing Jack, rubbing his chin. After about a minute Bill leans back slightly, crosses his legs knee to knee, swinging them away from Jack as he does so, and folds his arms tightly across his chest. Jack also notices that Bill has tightened his lips and that his respiration rate has increased. *What does Bill's body language signal and what would you advise Jack to do next?*
Bill began by listening to Jack (he was facing him) and considering what he was saying (rubbing his chin). Jack must then have said something to which Bill took exception, because he

suddenly exhibited signs of distancing himself (leaning back slightly), closing his posture (crossing his legs knee to knee, and folding his arms tightly across his chest; the last gesture, in this context, also signals that Bill is going to stick to his views), stifling something he wants to say (tightening his lips), and possibly losing his temper (increased respiration rate). It would be sensible for Jack to check his own body language. Has he for example been using any gestures to which Bill could have taken exception such as finger jabbing, or adopting an accusatory or sarcastic tone of voice. He should ensure that his own body language looks relaxed and receptive, and then stop and involve Bill in the conversation. Bill clearly has something he wants to say, so Jack should invite him to say it by remarking, for example, 'Bill, I can see that you're not happy with what I've said. Perhaps I didn't express myself very well. Put simply, I'm concerned about your decision to delegate much of the project work. Can we discuss it, please?'

Example 2

Jill is an energetic and forthright manager running a team of customer service clerks. She is talking to one of them, Peter, in her office. He is sitting in the visitor's chair and she is sitting on the corner of her desk on the same side as him. They are reviewing monthly statistics, and the conversation is going smoothly until Peter mentions that a team leader vacancy has arisen in the finance department; he was wondering how Jill would feel if he applied for it. Up until this point they had both been looking at pages of statistics that he had brought into Jill's office, and so he had been leaning forward looking at the figures or looking up to discuss them with Jill. As soon as he raised the matter of the vacancy however, his eyes only glanced at hers: they spent most of their time while asking the question looking at the carpet. He crossed his legs knee to knee and twined one of his feet behind the other leg; he sunk his head into his shoulders; his respiration rate increased and his voice became more hesitant; he also began 'washing' his hands. *What does Peter's body language signal and what would you advise Jill to do next?*

When Peter was talking about the statistics he seemed quite comfortable, but when the conversation turned to him and his relationship with Jill it changed dramatically. He gave off signs of being submissive (averting his gaze downwards and away from Jill, intertwining his legs, adopting a shrinking posture) and anxious (increased respiration rate – which probably affected his voice as his posture became more closed, wiping perspiration from his hands). All the signs are that he is very nervous about asking Jill this question and he has probably summoned up a lot of courage to do so. Perhaps the first thing that Jill should do is smile to signal that it is OK to ask the question and that she is happy that he did. Next, she should move away from her physically dominant position (sitting on the corner of her desk makes her taller than Peter), perhaps by pulling up another visitor's chair. If she returns to her own chair she should sit in it in her *usual* position regardless of the 'barrier' of the desk (to make a big thing out of moving her chair from its usual position would probably only make Peter even more anxious). Wherever she sits, she should face Peter with only the top half of her body; the bottom half should be pointed away from him. This is the type of position we unconsciously adopt when talking to friends, for example. She should also sit asymmetrically, again to signal relaxed informality. With luck he will begin to 'mirror' her posture and so relax himself. Finally Jill should involve him by probing why he is thinking of making the application, what he wants to achieve by doing so, and how she can help etc. To avoid sounding like an interrogator, especially as Peter is so nervous at the moment, she will need to smile, make eye contact perhaps only 50 per cent of the time and get him to talk by pausing while making encouraging, listening sounds such as 'Mmmm' and 'Uh-huh'.

Example 3

George is a newly appointed head-office personnel consultant working in a large company with autonomous divisions. He is visiting one of the divisions for the first time and is talking to the divisional personnel manager, Charles, in a meeting-room. Charles has arranged for the divisional chief executive to pop in at some stage so that George can be introduced to him. While the conversation has progressed Charles has gradually relaxed way back in his chair and is gesticulating freely, mainly with open palm gestures. His eye contact with George is direct, his state-ments factual, and his tone of voice pleasant. They are clearly getting on well and George is mirroring Charles' body language. The door opens and the divisional chief executive walks in. He motions that they need not get up as he introduces himself to George and shakes hands. Immediately, however, Charles shifts to an upright posture, clasping his hands in front of him on the table. Sharing his eye contact between George and the chief ex-ecutive he summarises the discussion so far, then leans back as the chief executive speaks with George. George notices that Charles is stroking his chin with one hand while the other hand is wrapped around his middle. His eyes are flicking rapidly be-tween George and the chief executive. *If you were George, what would you make of the situation and how would you react to it?*

The arrival of the chief executive has caused quite a change in Charles. Up to that point his posture, gestures, voice, and eye contact all said that he was very relaxed and enjoying the discus-sion. On the arrival of the chief executive, however, he quickly became very formal (his 'newsreader' posture) and once he had handed the meeting over to the chief executive and George, he became a mixture of thoughtful (hand rubbing chin) and anxious (arm cuddling his middle). He was also keenly interested in the reaction that George and the chief executive were having on each other (eyes flicking from one to the other rather than staying with the speaker, as one would expect). George could draw cer-tain conclusions from this reaction. First, that Charles had a very formal and hierarchical relationship with the chief executive, and second, that Charles had a high emotional stake in how the chief executive felt about the meeting. George might respond to these deductions by adopting a more upright, asymmetrical posture while staying reasonably relaxed and open, perhaps with one hand on the table and the other on the arm of his chair. Eye con-tact should be totally with the chief executive when listening to him and weighted in his favour when talking to him (that is, in-clude Charles with glances only). Listening should be obvious by the use of 'Mmmm' and 'Uh-huh' and also by the use of summaries, reflecting back, and probing to show interest. It is probably safest to ensure that the ratio of talking is in the chief executive's favour unless he shows that he wants to ask ques-tions. In summary George should take the cue from Charles and shift his body language from informal and relaxed to more formal with a hint of deference.

Summary

Body language is one of those subjects that can be tackled at different levels from the superficial to the deep. Superficially you need be aware only of major aspects such as eye contact and posture while in depth you can look even at the difference that individual finger positions can make. In this section I have given you an overview of what is important and, while trying to steer clear of the subtleties of hand-to-ear and hand-to-nose gestures, I have tried to sharpen your awareness of body language – both your own and other people's. I have focused on the sort of body language relevant to influencing situations rather than social situations, professional interrogations, and so on.

A vital point to remember is that most of the information that reaches our brain enters via the sense of sight. We pick up and process visual information very rapidly indeed, often without knowing that we have done so. Where there is a contradiction between what someone is telling us with their words and what they are inadvertently telling us with their body language it is the latter that we pay attention to every time. So by paying attention to eye contact, tone of voice, posture, proximity, and hand gestures we can not only reinforce our spoken words but we can also minimise the chances of inadvertently antagonising other people. By observing other people's body language we can assess how our words are being received and determine how best to approach those people. (If you want to find out more about this fascinating subject I can recommend *Body Language* (London, Sheldon Press, 1981) by Allan Pease.)

As a general guideline with which to end this section:

- Try to sit reasonably upright, leaning back slightly, in an asymmetrical position: you will look relaxed but attentive
- Make eye contact 50–70 per cent of the time, *especially* when you are making a statement or request that must have impact (see the following section on assertiveness)
- Keep your tone of voice neutral (but not a monotone) so that key words do not become lost in emotional overtones

- If you are a natural gesticulator, use more open-palm gestures than finger-pointing and -wagging gestures.

Assertiveness

Assertiveness is a subject with many facets. Although it has been seen traditionally as a way of enhancing the self-esteem and skills of people who were having difficulty handling life's problems it has emerged as a topic of relevance to management, leadership, teamwork, selling, negotiating, and of course influencing. Assertiveness can help us in many ways related to positive influencing. Here is a list:

- Being more persuasive
- Focusing on behaviour rather than personality
- Improving our tolerance of others when our underlying beliefs differ
- Protecting ourselves from the manipulative tactics that others may try to use against us.

In this section I shall give you an overview of assertiveness and then show you how it relates to the items on this list.

Assertiveness can be approached from a variety of directions but one of the most illustrative to begin with is the *fight-or-flight response*. This is the reaction that takes place within our bodies to prepare us for action when we are threatened. It is something bred in us over the millenia. Imagine a caveman or -woman strolling around a corner and coming face to face with a sabre-toothed tiger. If the caveman or -woman reacted casually to the danger they would get eaten. If on the other hand they were especially quick at clubbing the tiger or running away they would live to reproduce. The 'mechanism' that gets people ready to fight or to run is the fight-or-flight response.

When we are threatened, adrenalin is pumped into the bloodstream, causing a chain reaction. Acid increases in the stomach so that we can rapidly obtain the energy value of any food there; the heart beats faster, and the respiration rate increases. Combined with a dilation of blood-vessels in the muscles our physical strength and speed increase. The palms of the hands and soles of the feet perspire for better grip. Capillaries in the skin and bodily extremities contract to reduce the likelihood of bleeding, and the pain sensors are subdued. Certain mental functions such as decision making are intensified. All very useful stuff when you are faced with a sabre-toothed tiger. As I said, this fight-or-flight response has been bred into all of us. It is one of the main ways of coping with threatening situations. It even comes into play when faced with interpersonal conflict (sabre-toothed tigers being a bit thin on the ground these days).

We have another coping mechanism as well – our *verbal reasoning ability*. We can use our brains and our language to talk through conflict. Unfortunately it is not as simple as that; there is a problem. The prime place for learning how to resolve interpersonal conflict is in the family, as we grow. In our early years, however, there are three obstacles that combine to prevent us from becoming adept at resolving conflict with our verbal reasoning ability. The first is that in our formative years our verbal ability is undeveloped, so parents and older siblings have the edge on us. The second is that parents especially are like omnipotent giants to us. What they say goes. Whenever we are in conflict with them, they usually win, primarily because they are bigger than we are, can out-argue us, and can intimidate us by physically dominating us, invading our personal space, making excessive eye contact etc. The third obstacle is that opportunities for conflict are numerous because of all the rules, literal and assumed, that adults apply to children. The net result is that in the presence of persistent conflict with all-powerful, rule-making giants we receive more practice in our fight-or-flight response than we do in our verbal reasoning ability. There is significant evidence that even the offspring of kind, loving parents are on the receiving end of conflict – so much so that by the age of seven most of our repertoires for handling conflict have been learned, and they are more fight-or-flight than verbal reasoning. We carry these behavioural repertoires with us into adulthood, when we call them aggressive (fight), submissive (flight), and assertive (verbal reasoning). (As a brief aside, when people on my assertiveness courses query the 'repertoires learned by seven' statement, I often do two things. First, I point out that it is not only behaviours that are habit-forming but thoughts also. Second, I ask people to describe a recent situation in which they behaved either aggressively or submissively and to note down the thoughts that immediately preceded their behaviour; then, to state how a seven-year-old's thoughts would differ in exactly the same situation. There is usually no difference at all. Forty-seven-year-olds are just as capable as seven-year-olds of saying, 'This isn't fair' or 'I shan't be your friend any more'. They just dress it up in adult teminology.)

I should point out at this stage that the preceding paragraphs are really a rapid tour of assertiveness. We have not, for example, touched upon self-esteem, central to a lot of assertiveness theory. You have enough information though to appreciate the roots of our behaviour. As we grow we get more practised at aggressive and submissive behaviours than we do at assertive ones. We certainly see more examples and role models. But what to these three behaviours look like? I will describe them now. As you read the descriptions, please remember that we are talking more about responses to interpersonal conflict rather than relations between people when there is no conflict.

Aggressive behaviour

This is characterised by a desire to win even at the expense of others. In sport or selling, that might be acceptable or even desirable, but in normal relations it is wholly counterproductive, primarily because of the underlying attitudes. In general terms people who behave aggressively feel that they have more rights than other people, so they feel it is all right for them to bully and manipulate, or use sarcasm, swearing, and put-downs to get what they want. Sometimes their tactics are obvious and sometimes they are subtle. They use their body language to help them intimidate other people. They will physically dominate them, invade their personal space, make them feel uncomfortable with excessive eye contact, tone and volume of voice, shake index fingers at them, and so on. Often they get their way but it is a short-term victory. They get neither the help nor the co-operation of others which, unless they are some kind of hermit, is essential to personal as well as organisational effectiveness.

Submissive behaviour

The characteristic of submissive behaviour is a desire to avoid conflict even at the expense of oneself. In general terms people who behave submissively feel they have fewer rights than other people, so they see no course of action other than to give in. They are easily manipulated, bullied, cajoled and flattered into doing what other people want. They persistently put their needs a poor second place to the needs of others. When they do try to get what they want it is usually by seeking sympathy. They have a very low conflict-threshold and, when they experience conflict, adopt a 'shrinking', protective, and closed posture. They find eye contact difficult. Their voice is usually quiet and hesitant. They avoid conflict but pay a heavy price for doing so. They lose the respect of others and, more importantly, they lose respect for themselves.

Assertive behaviour

This is very well-balanced. It is characterised by a determination to stand up for one's own rights but, in doing so, to acknowledge the rights of others. A *genuinely* assertive person may therefore feel they have a right to be listened to, but that will make them more predisposed to listen to others. People who behave assertively are not easily intimidated. They tend to be straight, open, and honest. They verbalise their feelings when it is appropriate to do so. Their body language looks calm and confident. Their tone of voice and gestures support what they are saying rather than contradict it. In fact all the aspects of body language relating to eye contact, posture, tone of voice etc that I described in the last section as productive are all signs of assertiveness. Assertive people probe and listen a lot and, while they can stand their ground, they rarely use that ability to win at the expense of someone else. Finally they recognise that in most situations a win/win outcome is usually the best for all concerned. Consequently they earn respect and personal credibility.

To behave assertively you have to be able to do two things: *think assertively* and *use assertiveness techniques*. We will look first at thinking assertively.

Thinking assertively

Our behaviour is preceded by two separate events. The first is a *trigger.* This is usually something that someone says or does. It could be major, such as an upset customer appearing to blame us personally for their problem, or it could be minor, such as a well-intentioned person who does not understand the effect of jabbing a finger in our direction. The trigger sets off some *thoughts*, the second of the two events. For most of us the thoughts will be submissive or aggressive – 'This isn't fair. I always go to pieces when the boss speaks to me like that' or 'No one speaks to me like that and gets away with it'. Our thoughts are often prone to exaggeration or generalisation, which makes it more difficult to behave assertively, because our behaviour is geared more to our thoughts than it is to the outcome we want. This point must be emphasised. In conflict situations our behaviour is more likely to be the result of a self-fulfilling prophecy than deliberately chosen to achieve the outcome we want.

When we are not in control of our thoughts, and our thoughts determine our behaviour, we are *behaving by default.* What assertive people manage to do is to control their thoughts and think assertively so that they gear their behaviour to the outcome they want. This is behaving by design. Even though your thoughts are the one thing on this planet over which you could have total control, gaining that control is not easy. We have all had years if not decades of practice in thinking the way we do, and old habits are hard to break – especially if our basic beliefs run deep.

We all have a set of *basic beliefs* about ourselves, about situations, and about the way things should be. We acquired it during childhood and rarely question it because, to us, it is reality. Yet for most of us a thorough reappraisal of our early programming can open up new possibilities in the way we see ourselves, our abilities, our potential, our role in life, and many other previously taken-for-granted 'facts'. These beliefs affect the way we think which in turn affects the way we behave. When we take responsibility for our thoughts we take responsibility for our actions and start behaving more by design rather than by default. At this stage all we need to help us stay assertive, rather than drift into submissiveness or aggressiveness, are a few assertiveness techniques.

Assertiveness techniques

Before looking at the main assertiveness techniques, it is worth emphasising the importance of body language. The wrong tone of voice, for example, will turn your assertive words into aggressive ones; an avoidance of eye contact will turn your assertive statement into a submissive one. So in what follows please remember that the techniques need to be supported by the right body language. Here are the main techniques:

Basic assertion   This means saying what you want or how you feel – clearly. I have emphasised the word 'clearly' because that is where most people go wrong. They find it too easy to use emotive language and to ramble on. They seem to think that being honest means being so about everything they are thinking at the time. It does not. It means being honest about what is *relevant*. The other person might remind you of your uncle Albert on a bad day, Attilla the Hun, or an agitated kipper. It does not matter. If that information will hinder rather than help the situation, keep it yourself. 'That's just what my father used to do' is probably irrelevant but 'I wish you'd told me earlier. Telling me at this late stage will cause problems' probably is relevant. Sticking to what is relevant also helps with the other major aid to clarity – being concise.

Sometimes, to beef up our case or to defer the potential conflict (even if only by a few seconds) we ramble, beat about the bush, and overjustify. Pruning the words to the minimum – consistent with accuracy – never fails to assist clarity. Amazingly it also makes the words easier to say and to hear.

Broken record   The old saying, 'If at first you don't succeed, try, try again', neatly describes the broken record. It is as useful to submissive people, who might otherwise back down, as it is to aggressive people, who might escalate a situation. It consists of repeating what you want over and over again in response to someone else's attempts to manipulate you. Here is an example. Let us say a salesman is trying to make an appointment with you which you do not want. The conversation, using the broken record, might go like this:

– Hi! I'm Mr Pushy from WizBang Computers. I'd like to come and see you. May I make an appointment, please?
– I understand you want to see me but I don't want to make an appointment, thank you.

97

– Our computers use state-of-the-art technology and are really competitively priced. You'll love them.

– I'm sure I will, but I don't want to make an appointment, thank you.

– It's no trouble, honestly. I'm in your area on Tuesday. Would you prefer morning or afternoon?

– I'm sure it is no trouble but I don't want to make an appointment.

– I can offer very substantial discounts at the moment.

– I'm sure you can but I don't want to make an appointment.

– Why not?

– I just don't want to make an appointment.

– Oh . . . All right, then. May I send you some literature?

– Yes. That would be fine, but I don't want to make an appointment.

Notice that you never once tried to out-argue the salesman, neither were you rude. All you did was to acknowledge what he said and then repeat what it was you wanted, clearly and concisely, without reason or apology.

Initially some people feel a little uncomfortable saying the same thing over and over, so I usually make three points. First, if someone is trying to make you agree to something you would rather not agree to, the broken record is immovable and it has the real advantage that you do not even have to engage your brain. No one can out-argue you when you use the broken record. Second, you do not have to say exactly the same thing every time. You could say that you would like to help or you could suggest an alternative or whatever, but then you repeat the broken record at the end of every sentence. Finally, while you can use it to stand your ground you can also use it to encourage the other person to come to a compromise and, once you see them moving, you can move too. Such as when the boss wants you to work late:

– I need this done tonight before you go home.

– I have to be away on time tonight. Is there another way we could get it done?

– I want it done tonight.

– I'd do it if I could but I have to get away on time tonight.

I'll happily discuss other ways we can get it done.

– What's so important that means you have to leave at five o'clock?

– I have plans, so I can't do it, but I'll help work out an alternative.

– Well . . . Let's see what other ways there are then.

Pointing out a discrepancy   Imagine a situation where a manager has asked a word-processor operator to have a report finished by four o'clock. By ten past four it has not arrived. An aggressive manager would stride up to the operator, invade their personal space, and demand to know where it is; he would probably jump to a few conclusions as to why it was not ready. A submissive manager would wait until four-thirty and then approach the operator: 'Hello . . . it's only me. I hope I'm not being . . . er . . . a nuisance. I know how busy you are. I was . . . er . . . just wondering if . . . er . . . by any chance you had perhaps had a chance to look at that report I gave you this morning.' An assertive manager would ask – using eye contact, a pleasant posture and neutral tone of voice 'Hi, we agreed the report I gave you would be ready at four o'clock. It's now ten past four. Is there a problem?'

This approach points out a discrepancy. It consists of three elements: 'This is what we agreed would happen. This is what has happened. Why is that?' The discrepancy could be between the way things used to be and the way they are now, between what you expected to happen and what has happened, what you hoped to happen and what has happened, and so on. It helps you get straight to the point in a very non-accusatory way.

Pointing out a consequence   This is where you tell the other person what will happen if something else does not. 'If you won't agree to help me, I'll have to report you to your boss.' It is effectively a threat but it is not delivered in a threatening manner. Your body language must give no hint of a threat. It is actually much more effective if presented as a straightforward statement of cause and effect. It can also be 'sweetened' with a proposal of what you would like to happen: 'If you won't agree to help me, I'll have to report you to your boss. I'd prefer it if we could work something out between us.'

These are the main assertiveness techniques. If necessary you can combine them in a sequence that gets tougher and tougher but which stays consistently assertive. Here is an example of a conversation between two managers working on a project team together. One manager feels they need to discuss plans soon while the other sees no urgency:

– . . . So, because the main summer vacation period falls within the project period, I feel we need to meet this week to agree a schedule. Can we meet this week, please?

– I'm a bit busy right now. I'd like to put it off for a few weeks.

– I feel that will cause problems. I'd like to meet this week, please.

– We've got months for this project. What's the rush?

– I'm concerned about people taking vacations, so I'd like to agree a schedule. Can we meet this week please?

– I really don't have time.

– Time is a problem for everyone but I feel this project is complex enough to warrant priority. You seem not to. Why is that – because I'd still like to meet this week.

– I just don't see it as that urgent.

– I'm afraid I do, so I'd still like to meet this week.

– I couldn't see you until the week after next at the earliest.

– That's unfortunate because I feel that this project is important. If you can't meet me I'll have to tell the boss that he can't have the schedule yet, and why. I'd prefer not to have to do that, so can we meet this week?

– Oh . . . all right.

Assertiveness can help us influence in a variety of ways. Here are the main ones:

- *It makes us more persuasive.* Being direct and honest about what is relevant tends to have more impact than antagonising people with emotive comparisons, or rambling on, deferring the crunch point. The broken record opens many doors owing to its persistency. Pointing out discrepancies and consequences helps address matters directly and accurately.
- *It helps focus on behaviour rather than personality.* Assertive

people tend to understand more about the trigger/thoughts/behaviour sequence of events than non-assertive people. Consequently in situations where they want to modify someone else's behaviour they are more likely to control and use their own behaviour so that it forms the appropriate trigger to assertive behaviour in the other person.

- *It increases our tolerance of others.* Increased tolerance comes to assertive people from a variety of sources. One is that they do not see social interaction as a trial of strength. They prefer a win/win to a win/lose outcome. The number of things on which they are prepared to stand firm or on which they hold black-and-white opinions is usually lower after assertiveness training than before. Individual differences are tolerated. Another source of their tolerance is that they are less inclined to influence negatively by the packaging (body language, terminology etc) around a message. They know that other people are only human, may get emotional about conflict, and, in those circumstances, are unlikely to choose their words and body language carefully. So they are less susceptible to 'packaging' as a trigger to inappropriate behaviour. Instead they go straight to the message. Finally, they realise that while there may be significant overlap beliefs differ from person to person and that if their own 'reality' is the result of early programming then so is other people's. That all adds up to greater tolerance in many areas, without compromising essential ones.

- *It protects us from other people's attempts to manipulate us.* We know that when some people try to influence us they do not do so positively but manipulatively. The effect on most people is to stimulate their emotions so that their thoughts go awry and they behave aggressively, or submissively. One of the benefits of assertiveness training is that we can put a wedge between what other people are saying and how we are feeling. Basic assertion and the other techniques provide such a wedge. So do probing and reflecting. Think back to the last time someone tried a 'put-down' on you. How did you react? Did it make you feel hurt or vulnerable? Or did it make you feel like counter-attacking with an equally barbed comment? Now imagine the effect had you just remained untouched by it, maintained an open posture, a calm and neutral tone of voice, eye contact and probed into why they said what they did. The effect is usually very satisfying!

Summary

Like body language, assertiveness is one of those subjects that pervades all aspects of face-to-face communication. Most of us, even many senior managers, need to be more assertive. Most of us spend too much time being either submissive or aggressive. Both these types of behaviour have more disadvantages than advantages because they are based on the sort of characteristics we do not like in people. Assertiveness, on the other hand, is based on the characteristics that we do value in others. When you think of the characteristics of your best-ever boss, colleague, subordinate, neighbour, friend, and so on you are probably identifying assertiveness characteristics. The ability to be straight, open, and honest combined with an ability to listen and to be tolerant with us when we fail to choose our words carefully are characteristics we value in other people. It really does follow therefore that other people will value them in us too.

Our early upbringing, however, rarely helps us. Although we have the ability to reason our way verbally through conflicts we learn our reactions to such problems at a time when our verbal reasoning ability is not very well developed. Add to this the fact that our brains do not distinguish between physical and emotional threats when they pump adrenalin into our bloodstreams, and you can see why we revert more readily to the fight-or-flight response with which we are all endowed. These responses become habitual at a very early age and are carried with us into adulthood. They make it more difficult to influence other people positively.

Assertiveness, however, makes it easier to influence others and to make them feel good in the process. Not only is it non-manipulative (if used properly), it also makes it easier for us to resist attempted manipulation by others.

No-noes

In addition to the skills and behaviours that will help you be more influential it will be helpful if you are also aware of the behaviours that do more harm than good. So now we will turn our attention to the behaviours that could make you a worse influencer.

Talking more than listening

There are two reasons why this is unproductive. First, anyone who talks more than listens discovers less about the other person. They understand less about their situation, their priorities, the constraints within which they have to work, and so on. They understand less about what the other person will buy and so understand less how to sell their product to them. Second, when someone tries to dominate an influencing situation they are usually trying to manipulate. So at worst they are resorting to trickery and at best they are a bore. Even in social situations where influencing might be the last thing on someone's mind, we rarely warm to people who dominate a conversation (unless they happen to be exceedingly entertaining). Far better to probe and listen. You can then use your words sparingly – but deliberately and accurately nonetheless.

Using 'red rag' words and phrases

These are words and phrases that have no persuasive effect whatsoever and, worse, they irritate or antagonise the other person. Most people are aware of the saying, 'It was like a red rag to a bull'. We know that if we dangle a red rag in front of a bull we will antagonise it. Poor influencers persistently dangle 'red rag' words and phrases in front of the person they are trying to influence, often with the best of intentions, but all they do is antagonise. When someone begins a sentence 'With respect . . .' there is a good chance they are about to insult us. If they begin the sentence with the words 'With all due respect . . .' then we can be certain they are about to insult us! Similarly 'I hear what you say, but . . .' usually means that they have no intention of listening to us. Words such as 'generous', 'fair' and 'reasonable' can also backfire on us. If we say, 'This is a very generous offer' or, 'I'm being very reasonable about this' our influencing potential is diminishing. If the other person thought our offer generous or reasonable they would have snapped it up, so these words only serve to accuse them of being ungenerous and unreasonable. Even the word 'obviously' has an irritating propensity. 'Obviously everyone understands this point' or 'Obviously we can't pay that much' are redundant sentences. If everyone really does understand the point or already knows that you cannot pay that much there is no need to say it. If on the other hand they do not you have just irritated them or possibly even insulted them.

Making assumptions on other people's behalf is another good way of antagonising them. 'What you don't seem to realise is . . .' or 'What you have failed to take account of is . . .' are both sentences that will only annoy the other person, and the validity of the point you are making will be lost. 'Red rag' words and phrases need to be avoided. Their use is often habitual and unintentional, so be prepared to persevere.

Making counter-proposals

The worst time to make a proposal is when the other person is wondering why we are not considering theirs. There are two reasons why we fall into this trap. The first is that we genuinely do not like their proposal and so we deliver our own. The second is that their proposal triggers a good idea in our minds which we just blurt out. Either way, we are on a different wavelength from the other person. They are geared up to discuss their proposal. No matter how good our proposal we are attempting to sow it on stony ground. The conversation can even degenerate into a kind of verbal ping-pong. Far better to discuss their proposal. Ask questions about it to encourage them to think it through and to signal that you do not readily accept it, then present your proposal in the form of a hypothetical question.

Facilitating defend/attack spirals

When we human beings are attacked we tend to react either by being very defensive or by counter-attacking. It is a natural human trait. It also causes problems for influencers. The first is that, because it is a natural human trait, it tends to be reciprocated: they attack, you defend. Your defence comes across as a counter-attack and so they have to respond appropriately. The second problem is that even a denial of an allegation can be seen as a counter-attack. Either way, before you know where you are, you are in a defend/attack spiral – down! The only workable course of action is to be totally solution-oriented. So even if an allegation is made against you it will be sensible to respond only briefly and to move on quickly towards a solution without waiting for a counter-response.

Stacking up arguments in your favour

Logic tells us that the more reasons we can give someone for doing something the stronger our case must be and, consequently, the more unassailable our position. In reality the reverse is true. This is so because, first, it sounds as if we are making excuses rather than giving reasons. If we have to give that many reasons, the logic goes, the case must be very weak indeed, otherwise it would not need such bolstering. Second, all the other person has to do is tackle our weakest reason and the rest either lose credibility or tumble like a row of dominoes. Imagine asking a colleague for a lift home, something which they have done in the past, but this time their response is, 'I'm sorry, I can't tonight: I promised I'd be home early, and I'm a bit short on petrol, and the engine is making a funny noise, and I'm hoping to sell it soon so I'm trying to keep the mileage down, and I'm not sure how to get to my house from your neighbourhood.' Wouldn't it be more convincing if they just said, 'I'm sorry, I can't tonight: I promised I'd be home early'? Far better, therefore, to have one strong reason or argument in your favour and stick to it.

Persistent use of the 'royal we'

Let me say, to begin with, that there are situations when you can and should use 'we'. If for example you were representing your organisation to some external business or individual 'we' would be acceptable. If you were talking about a collective decision or response 'we' would be the only accurate pronoun to describe whose decision or response it is. If you mean both you and the person to whom you are talking 'we' is obvious. I have seen numerous discussions however where someone attempts to add weight to their argument by saying 'we' instead of 'I'.

Appraisal discussions are a good example. I sometimes hear appraising managers say, '*We* feel that you aren't quite ready for promotion' or, '*We* felt that you hadn't quite grasped the importance of that part of the project.' The effect is always the same. First, it drives a wedge between the appraiser and the appraisee. The appraiser is effectively saying, 'I am a chief and you are an indian so don't try to disagree with my assessment of your performance.' In modern organisations this is just the sort of division that stifles commitment. Second, it sets off a thought process in the appraisee's mind: if appraisers have to hide behind the corporate 'we' then either their case must be very weak indeed or they lack the courage of their convictions.

People also hide behind the corporate 'we' when they do not want to do something. '*We* couldn't possibly agree to that' usually means 'I'd have to take a decision by myself. That means sticking my neck out. I'd rather not.'

If by your terminology you set up the thought process in the other person's mind that you are seeking something to hide behind or to bolster your case you are, ironically, giving them confidence and so hindering your own attempts to influence them. So whether your use of the 'royal we' is habit from a bygone age or a kind of security blanket it is far better to reserve it for the situations in which it is appropriate.

Using 'formalspeak'

Another phenomenon that never ceases to amaze me is people's tendency to seek comfort from official language – formalspeak. Here is an example. Although the person using it would not necessarily be doing so for reasons of psychological comfort it does illustrate what I mean by formalspeak. Imagine you have a friend who is a typical British bobby. He is telling you about a recent arrest. 'I was walking down the High Street when I spotted this chap. "Hallo," I thought to myself, "he's up to no good." I watched him for a bit and, sure enough, he was about to do over the bank, so I nabbed him.' Normal, everyday language for this typical British bobby chatting to a friend. He then goes into court to give evidence and his words turn into formalspeak: 'I was proceeding along the High Street when I noticed the accused acting in a suspicious manner. I continued my observations until such time as my suspicions proved accurate and then I proceeded to effect an arrest.' Why did the bobby not talk to you like this? Put simply, it is so formal that to do so would have altered your perception of the conversation.

I have observed many people who, when placed in a stressful situation, however mild, alter their terminology from informal to formal. The selection interviewer who begins every question with 'Can you tell me . . .?' instead of just asking the question; the trade union official who keeps saying 'My members have instructed me, in relation to the aforementioned matter, to seek . . .' instead of 'What we want is . . .'; and the accountant who points out 'an unexplainable variance in the cost and revenue estimates' instead of saying, 'the figures don't add up'. Whatever the reason for unexplained formalspeak the effect is always the same. It creates 'distance' from the other person, making a meeting of minds less likely. It also signifies unease with the situation that the other person may seek to exploit.

One final point: formalspeak can be very subtle. When a videoed discussion on a course has gone a little 'frosty', and no one can explain why, the video replay will often show that everyday terminology such as 'can't' and 'don't' have changed to the more correct 'cannot' and 'do not'. The change sends a small but unmistakable signal of how the speaker was feeling, and that signal was picked up by the other person.

Summary

As well as consciously employing productive behaviours we need to avoid the counter-productive ones. In particular we need to listen rather than talk, avoid 'red rag' words and phrases, and resist the temptation to make counter-proposals and trigger off defend/attack spirals. We also need to give a single, compelling reason for something rather than stack up arguments in our favour. We also need to avoid inappropriate use of the 'royal we' and resist the comfort of formalspeak.

Manipulation and how to resist it

As well as avoiding the counter-productive behaviours, there may also be occasions when you need to avoid the manipulative tactics that some people employ. Have you ever made a decision or agreed to something and afterwards felt as if you had been painted into a corner? Uncomfortable though it was, the decision appeared to be the only viable alternative at the time yet, afterwards, you had this nagging suspicion that, were you in that position again, you would make a different decision. If you have felt like that then you have probably been on the receiving end of manipulation.

As you know from Chapter 2 on fundamental principles manipulation might be an effective form of influencing in the short term but it produces antagonism and resentment for the future. As well as attempting to resist the manipulation tactics of other people it will therefore be better for all concerned if you can encourage them to be straight with you. To help, I have listed the main manipulation tactics that you are likely to encounter together with simple but effective counter-measures. The first few tactics are common in the sales world, so I have used sales examples to illustrate them, but you will also find them in non-sales situations.

Keeping you waiting

This is a tactic that senior people use on junior people and buyers use on sales representatives. It is a way of saying, 'I'm calling the tune around here because I'm the more important person.' Their hope is that you will either stew a little while you are waiting and so become more nervous or that the effect on your schedule will cause you to feel under pressure and so you will agree to what they want in order to keep the discussion short. An effective counter-measure, assuming you do not want to reschedule the meeting, is to always keep some work with you. (I keep a back-reading file in my briefcase containing magazine articles I have already scanned and want to read in more detail. This file, incidentally, also proves its worth when you are faced with delays in public transport, traffic jams, and so on.) That way their attempt at pressure becomes a gift of time in which you did some work that you would not otherwise have done. Alternatively you can use the time for some last-minute preparation. I find it useful for a last-minute dress rehearsal in my mind of the opening of the meeting or the handling of any particularly tricky bits. Finally, if the time available for the meeting becomes too squeezed you may have no alternative but to reschedule. If their delay was genuinely unavoidable, they will understand; if it was an attempt to manipulate you, they will see it has not worked and be less inclined to try it on you in the future.

The best offer

Picture the scene. The young sales rep enters Mr Big's office. He was up half the night ensuring that his sales pitch is word perfect. He is no more than 30 seconds into it when Mr Big's secretary comes through on the intercom with a pre-arranged message. 'Hello, Mr Big. Mr High-and-Mighty wants to see you in two minutes in his office.' What can Mr Big do other than apologise and say, 'Well, let's skip the haggling, just give me your best price.' He also lets slip, for good measure, that he has one of the sales rep's competitors coming in this afternoon. And what can the sales rep do but go straight to his fall-back price. Whether you are negotiating a price for a product, the start date for a project, or how many staff you can temporarily second to another department, watch out if the other party puts you under unexpected time pressure and attempts to push you straight to your bottom line.

The sales rep could respond, 'I'd like to give you my best price but until I've learned more about your requirements, I don't know what my best price is.' At best that response will make Mr Big realise that pushing the sales rep is not the most sensible route to the best deal and, at the very least, it should let Mr Big know that he is not dealing with a push-over. Side-stepping the request and signalling that you need information is a good counter-measure. Interestingly, in this response, you have not disagreed with the other person. In fact you have done the reverse: you have agreed that you want to give them what they want. It is just that you cannot do it the way they have suggested.

The principal ploy

A favourite tactic in buying situations, the principal ploy is also found in multidisciplinary project teams. In buying situations the sales rep is getting close to his bottom line when he discovers that the person to whom he is talking does not have the authority to sign the order. The buyer leaves the room and returns five minutes later saying that his boss will not sign the order unless another x per cent discount is given. The buyer gets the x per cent, disappears again, and returns five minutes later saying that his boss wants delivery in two weeks instead of four. The unseen principal always wants a bit more. Sometimes only the threat of consulting a principal is enough. In management/union negotiations you will hear the phrase, 'My members will never agree to that' or 'The board of directors would never accept that.'

In multidisciplinary teams, the accountant will have to check with the finance director, or the marketing manager will have to check with the marketing director on anything they do not like and they will bring their 'principal's' demands to the discussion.

When the principal ploy is used against you effective counter-measures are first, to insist on discussing matters with the principal directly or, second, resurrect matters that the other party thought were already agreed. 'If you want delivery in two weeks and an x per cent discount we'll have to take another look at quantity.' That works just as well in non-sales situations. Furthermore with this counter-measure you are not only side-stepping the attempted manipulation but also effectively encouraging the other person to be open and honest. That way you can arrive at an agreement with which you both feel comfortable.

The subsidiary decision

Here is an example. If you are unsure whether to buy a certain car or not, the sales person may ask you which colour you would prefer if you were to buy one. 'Red? Let me see if we have one in stock . . . Yes, I could have that ready for you tomorrow. Would you prefer delivery in the morning or the afternoon?' By asking you to make small decisions he is making the assumption that the big decision is already made. Waiver on a purchase decision in a shop and the sales assistant might ask, 'How do you prefer paying for items like this, cash or terms? – Terms? . . . Let me see what the monthly repayments would be.' It is a pushy way of selling and it is a method of manipulation favoured by pushy people.

'I need to borrow one of your staff. Would you prefer to lend me Bill or Sally?' assumes that the decision whether to lend a member of staff at all has already been made. The only effective counter-measure is to keep your wits about you and remind them that the small decisions will only be made after the big decision. You are not refusing to help. It is just that you want to make the decision in your own way and in your own time. Use assertive language, good eye-contact and a neutral tone of voice and they will not try it on you again in a hurry. The effect is once more to teach them that if they want to influence you they will stand a better chance of doing so openly and honestly rather than manipulatively.

These four manipulation tactics are most common in the sales world, although you will see them elsewhere. The remainder are more common outside sales situations.

Making you feel guilty or responsible

Let us say that a colleague wants a lift home. His car is being repaired and he does not want to miss his child's birthday party, which he probably will do if he uses public transport. You do not want to give him a lift because you want to be home in good time too. After several attempts to persuade you to agree, which you have resisted, he says, 'Well . . . because of you, I'll miss my little girl's birthday party. Boy, will she be upset.' People do this to each other all the time. You cannot let me have the figures when I want them so I'll miss my deadline. It is your fault. You cannot help me with something as I had hoped, which means that I will have to alter my plans. The inconvenience is your fault.

The best counter-measure is to think assertively and not to let other people make you feel guilty about standing up for your rights or to feel responsible for the predicament they have made for themselves. They may have a right to ask for your help but you may have a right to refuse it – without feeling guilty. The alternative is to allow other people to choose how *you* feel – and

111

most of us would struggle in vain to see any sense in that!

Making you feel inadequate

Closely allied to making you feel guilty is making you feel inadequate. This is usually achieved through sarcasm, patronisation, and put-downs. By denting your self-esteem people use this technique to make you more malleable. Again, assertiveness thinking and assertiveness techniques come to the rescue.

First, you make the decision that no one will determine how you feel. Your thoughts are the one thing on this planet over which you can have total control if you so choose. The second step is to use one of two very simple but effective techniques. *Probing* is the easier of the two. You simply probe into what they have said. 'That colour makes you look all sickly' could cause you never to wear it again (flight) or to tell the other person that they have the dress sense of a colour-blind gorilla (fight). It is far more effective however to ask, 'In what way?' If their comment is genuine, albeit badly expressed, they will elaborate, giving you valuable information. If it is designed to make you feel inadequate, they will back off.

The other technique is to *acknowledge* what they have said with a simple 'Yes, it does', and leave it at that. This may sound really strange but it is very, very effective. It is verbal judo, in which a small person can 'throw' a larger one by using their weight and momentum against them. Your 'attacker' is stopped in their tracks.

Acknowledging has another use, too. Imagine you are on the receiving end of a customer complaint. The customer is upset, has exaggerated their description of the problem, and appears to hold you personally responsible. You can *acknowledge* what they have said by using more rational and less emotive language than they have used and then go on to gather more information or to propose a solution. This is much more productive than becoming defensive or counter-attacking in some way. You are demonstrating that you have been listening and encouraging them to join you in seeking a solution.

Probing and acknowledging have another and significant, benefit when someone is trying to make you feel inadequate. They form a barrier between what the other person is saying and what you are feeling. That makes it easier for you to stay in control of your feelings and emotions and so behave by design rather than behave by default.

Using spurious logic

I once heard someone say that logic is what other people use to prove that you are wrong and, when it comes to manipulation, they were exactly right. Imagine a department in which the work is being restructured. One of the supervisors will be losing some of her more interesting cases and taking on a number of more routine ones. She is trying to persuade the manager to reconsider. After all rational attempts fail she asks, 'How would you like it if someone came along and made your job more boring?', to which the manager replies, in the only way he can, 'I wouldn't'. The supervisor then nods a satisfying nod as if to say, 'Well there you are then: case proven.'

The 'logic' is that if the manager would not like to have his job altered in this way he should not alter the supervisor's this way either. It rests on the invalid assumption that there is similarity between the manager and the supervisor, and between their two jobs: so if it would be wrong to change one of them it would be equally wrong to change the other. In the heat of debate this technique can be very powerful. It is only with hindsight that we leave the discussion with a nagging doubt.

The best counter-measure is to use probing. It not only forces the other person to justify their logic while signalling that you are only open to persuasion from sound reason and fact, it also buys you a significant amount of thinking time because you can think much faster than they can talk.

Review

We began this chapter by looking at probing and listening. *Probing* I described as the most useful and versatile skill, the universal tool in your interpersonal skills tool-kit. Some types of probe such as open questions are very productive and quite safe to use generally. Others, such as closed and forced-choice questions, have more specific uses and need more careful handling. Others such as leading and evaluative questions are usually counter-productive and best avoided. *Listening* I described as the other side of the probing coin because the most productive form of listening is active rather than passive. To listen actively you probe, check understanding, summarise, and look as if you are listening.

I said that *getting on the same wavelength* was important because our brains perform a very efficient recognition function and, having done so, filter the information they receive accordingly. As it is very difficult influencing someone with whom you cannot communicate effectively it is important that we assist clarity. We can do so by signposting, checking our understanding, asking questions, disclosing relevant feelings (as long as we do not overdo it) and defusing emotive language. In group discussions we can augment these behaviours by managing the discussion process in such a way that participants adopt the same mode of thinking at the same time (positive, negative, factual, emotional etc).

I began *persuasive selling* by pointing out that customers, not salespeople, make purchase decisions; that customers buy to meet a need; and that customers buy benefits rather than features. I then explained how successful salespeople (of the non-manipulative variety) use a probing sequence to discover what customers want to buy and what will persuade them to buy it. I then made the point that if we, just like salespeople, want positively to influence people and sustain our relationship with them into the future they need to be happy with both the decision they have made and the process by which they made it. We can therefore use the round-up/reason/result sequence with the same effect as a non-manipulative salesperson. We also looked at the results of research into selling and negotiating and saw a lot of confirmation of the usefulness of the material covered so far.

In the section relating to *body language* we established that it had to support what we were saying. If it contradicted our words the non-verbal message would eclipse the spoken one. We also established that people who are not aware of body language let their 'non-verbals' come out unedited and so, if we look for the signs, we can increase our understanding of what they are thinking. But only if we look for clusters and timely changes. To influence someone positively we need to pay special attention to eye contact, tone of voice, posture, proximity, and gestures.

When we looked at assertiveness I made the point that truly assertive people do not just assert themselves. They listen a lot and are actually quite tolerant. This is partly owing to the fact they believe that if they have the right to be listened to then other people have that right too, and partly owing to the fact that, because their self-esteem is reasonably robust, they do not see the need to be too defensive.

The concept of learnt behaviour becoming habit is central to assertiveness. Unfortunately, during our formative years, our verbal reasoning ability is not yet developed and so we revert to our fight-or-flight response whenever we experience conflict. Because as children we live in a land of giants and are subject to numerous rules, conflict can happen frequently so the application of our fight-or-flight response to relationships gets a lot of practice. That practice leads to habitual behaviours that we carry with us into adulthood and that can be triggered by anything our brains perceive as a threat.

The result is that far too often we behave by default rather than by design. In conflict situations our behaviour is more likely to be the result of a self-fulfilling prophecy than to be chosen deliberately to achieve the outcome we want. To gain control of our behaviour, therefore, we need first to gain control of our thoughts. Once we are thinking assertively we can use assertiveness techniques more effectively.

Finally, we looked at some *no-noes*: the behaviours we sometimes think, albeit incorrectly, make us more persuasive or which make us feel more comfortable in influencing situations. They are usually all counter-productive and are best avoided. We also looked at some typical ways in which people may try to manipulate you and how you can counter their attempts.

Pause for thought

Before we move on, you may like to pause for thought and consider to what extent you currently use the core skills. In Table 3.2 are 10 questions. Please answer them honestly and see if they point towards any areas in which you would benefit from improvement.

Table 3.2
Core skills – questionnaire

How often do you:	Rarely	Sometimes	Often
1. talk more than you listen?	☐	☐	☐
2. feel that the other person is talking about things you feel are irrelevant?	☐	☐	☐
3. feel that your understanding and that of the other person are getting further apart rather than closer together?	☐	☐	☐
4. share with the other person what you are thinking or feeling?	☐	☐	☐
5. genuinely seek to understand the other person so that you can present your case in terms they will appreciate?	☐	☐	☐
6. consciously manage your own body language and observe that of the other person?	☐	☐	☐
7. make assumptions from one, isolated gesture or movement?	☐	☐	☐
8. find that your behaviour is more of a response to your emotions rather than a considered action leading towards a positive outcome?	☐	☐	☐
9. help other people speak up for themselves even if you disagree with them?	☐	☐	☐
10. feel that you have been pushed, coerced, or tricked into doing something?	☐	☐	☐

Preview

In the next chapter you will find three examples of situations where people are trying to influence someone else, along with a commentary relating to the core skills.

——— 4 ———
Bringing It Together

In the preceding chapters we looked at five fundamental principles and five core skills. For ease of reference we looked at them
individually. In reality, however, many of them overlap. Probing
was for example discussed in its own right yet it is also central to
persuasive selling; eye contact was discussed in the section on
body language yet it is also relevant to assertiveness and to listening. So in this chapter I want to show you what the principles
and skills look like in practice.

Three examples follow. The first concerns resolving conflict;
the second, informal appraisal; and the third, giving bad news to
someone. Along with the dialogue I have provided a commentary so that you can relate what is happening in the dialogue to
the principles and skills. Before you read the examples it is
worth bearing in mind the advantages and disadvantages of illus-
trating the learning points this way. On the one hand it is possible to concoct situations that demonstrate exactly what we want
to illustrate. On the other hand they are subject to your own perceptions. Everyone who reads them will automatically relate the
situations to their own experience, to people they know, and to
environments with which they are familiar. The example might
show someone saying, 'Jenkins, I wonder if I might trouble you
for a moment. Could you possibly spare a minute? I'd like a
quick word – in private, if that's all right'; but if in your organisation people would say, 'Jenkins, haul yourself in here. Boy, am I
gonna bust your ass!', the example will not feel real. A bit extreme, I know, but it makes the point. As you read the examples,
therefore, please treat them as illustrations of the principles and
skills and not as cast-iron recommendations for each and every
such situation in every environment you will come across.

Example one

ABC Metals is a large engineering company employing several

thousand people on 10 sites. During the last few years the number of staff in typical 'head-office' functions has been reduced considerably and everyone is fully stretched. Two years ago the company introduced a 'quality' programme based on the concept of internal customers. Initial results were better than expected but there are signs that it is now running out of steam. Phil, the operations director responsible for staff on all the sites, has asked Jane, the training manager, to come up with proposals for revitalising the quality programme. As both staff and budgets are tight Jane has proposed a combination of distance learning and cascade training through line managers. This differs from Phil's expectation of the training department running a series of programmes on every site. He has called Jane into his office to tell her that her proposals are unacceptable.

Phil is seated behind his vast desk reading through Jane's proposal, deliberately making Jane wait. She is sitting on the visitor's chair directly opposite. Eventually, Phil speaks. 'Jane,' he says, steepling his fingers in front of himself. 'Thank you for your proposal. It's clear that you've put a lot of effort into it. I've given it a great deal of thought but I'm afraid I'm going to have to insist that the training department does what we're paying you for and run these programmes yourself.'

Making someone wait is usually a deliberate pressure ploy. Combined with the seating positions and the steepled fingers, it indicates that Phil sees himself as very superior. Jane should be aware, therefore, that she needs to tread carefully.

Jane maintains a neutral expression. She is facing Phil with her legs crossed, knee to knee. Her legs are pointing slightly away from Phil and her hands are clasped loosely on the notepad on her lap. 'Thank you, Phil. I did work hard on it. What is it about it that you don't like?'

Jane's posture is relaxed, attentive and non-challenging. She acknowledges Phil's compliment, by-passes his statement, resists the temptation to defend her proposal, and proceeds to gather information.

Phil leans back in his executive chair and clasps his hands behind his head, crossing his legs, ankle to knee. 'My managers are very busy, you know. Apart from that, they're not trainers. They're engineers. They're no good at this soft-skill stuff like delivering a training course. That's your area. It's the kind of thing that you women are good at. So I'd like you to organise and run the programmes yourself,' he concludes with a smile.

Phil adopts the classic 'top dog' posture and then proceeds to patronise Jane (a thinly veiled form of aggression). Again she does not rise to the bait.

'Everyone in Training is good at running programmes,' responded Jane. 'It's part of the selection criteria. I'd like to make sure that I understand you, though. What are you aiming for with these programmes?'

She acknowledges, to show that she has heard, and signposts that she is about to ask a question to check her understanding. This helps keep Phil on her wavelength.

Phil leans forward, clasping his hands on his desk. 'I want to revitalise the quality programme. It started off exceptionally well but now it's run out of steam. If we're to meet our targets we need to rekindle the enthusiasm that was there at the beginning.'
'So it's a question of targets?' asks Jane.
'Precisely,' replies Phil. 'The holding company is breathing down our necks. There are rumours that unless we improve our position this year we could be up for sale and heaven knows what that would mean for all our jobs.'

By resisting the temptation to go down the fight-or-flight route, Jane has stayed in control of herself and is gaining control of the conversation. By probing and reflecting she is 'rounding up' useful information which is gradually highlighting what benefits Phil will buy into, as long as he can see the cause and effect between what he wants and what Jane is proposing.

'Yes, that would concern us all. Let me ask, though, in what way you feel the programme would be better if it was run by the training department as opposed to the methods described in my proposal?'

So far, Jane has not made a single statement about her proposal; she is still gathering information.

'I am concerned, Jane, that my managers are not trainers. Their presentations would lack impact and the programme would be discredited as a result. I do not see how we could possibly allow it.' Phil fixes Jane with a long stare as if to emphasise his point.

'May I summarise, to make sure I understand?' asks Jane.

'Sure,' replies Phil.

'You see this quality programme as an essential element of ABC's response to tough conditions and, in view of rumours about the holding company's intentions, you want to revitalise it. You're concerned, however, that any courses we run have to have the right impact because you want them to be credible amongst site staff and you feel that that credibility will come more readily from the training department than from your own managers.'

*Phil is starting to feel a bit uneasy now. His language has become slightly more formal. He is saying words such as 'are not' and 'do not' in full, whereas up to this point he has been happy to abbreviate them. Spotting the change in Phil's mood Jane signposts that she is about to check her understanding. This reassures Phil that she is not disagreeing. Jane uses the summary to paraphrase some of Phil's words so that they are both accurate **and** lend themselves to the points that she wants to make.*

Throughout Jane's summary Phil looks at her intently, nodding and making 'agreeing' sounds such as 'Yes' and 'Uh-huh'. He then says, 'Yes, that's how I feel, exactly.'

Jane knows from Phil's body language that her summary is being accepted – something he confirms with his words.

'How would you feel,' continues Jane, 'if I said that programmes like this one often fail where they are seen to come from the think-tank at head office? On the other hand if they are seen to be owned by the very people who make them work they stand a much better chance of success.'

Phil now leans back in his chair slightly and puts a hand up to his chin. Jane carries on, 'I agree that the credibility of the presenters is vital. However, I feel that the credibility of the programme itself is even more critical, and that will only come if it is owned by the operations department. My suggestion is that, to give the programme the best chance of success, we look at how to give your managers the impact they'll need when they present the programmes. I believe that's the only way forward if we want the benefits to be visible to the holding company.'

Jane wants to make a proposal but knows that she still needs to involve Phil with a suggestion, partly because of his seniority and partly because she wants him to think through what she is saying.

Phil's hand-to-chin gesture and posture indicate that he is considering what Jane is saying so she feels that she can now be more assertive. She uses self-disclosure to make her point.

As Jane delivers this last point she ensures she has direct eye contact with Phil, who continues rubbing his chin and eventually says, 'Tell me how you'd go about doing that.'

Eye contact adds considerably to Jane's point. Meanwhile we can see from his chin rubbing that Phil is considering seriously what Jane has said and is interested in finding out more.

It would have been easy in this example for Jane to have been intimidated by Phil's 'power play' – the way he used his vast desk, the waiting ploy, his apparent insistence, and his patronisation. She could have gone down the flight route and given in immediately, or she could have gone down the fight route, counter-attacking with a blistering defence of her proposal. Instead she ignored the 'packaging', avoided the triggers, and began rounding up information. This enabled her to identify what Phil would be prepared to buy into; all she had to do was to

establish in Phil's mind the cause and effect between her proposal and what Phil wanted. To do so she had to move at Phil's
pace, not her own. She took great care therefore to ensure that
they stayed on the same wavelength, and she adjusted her pace
according to signals coming from Phil's non-verbal communication.

Example two

Jack is manager of an administration department consisting of
three separate teams of 12 clerks. Each team has a team leader.
The work of each team is primarily routine, clerical tasks, and
motivation depends heavily on the approach of the team leaders.
One team leader, Sarah, was appointed six months ago. She was
promoted from within her team and, although she is substantially
older than the rest of the team, proved to be a very popular
choice. This is because she was a bit of a 'mother figure' and
spokesperson for the younger team members and also because,
having done the job for years, she is easily the most knowledgeable. Unfortunately morale has declined significantly in recent
months with implications for timekeeping, short-term absen-
teeism, and productivity. Jack has only just become aware of the
problem because he has been seconded to a project team for the
last two months. That secondment has now ended. He has heard
that morale is deteriorating because Sarah has been managing
autocratically, insisting that everything is done her way only, and
because she has been very pedantic about unimportant detail.

Jack has regular three-monthly appraisal discussions with his
team leaders. Sarah's is just about to begin.

Jack and Sarah sit at a round table in one of the company's
meeting-rooms. If the table were a clock-face, Jack would be at
the nine and Sarah at the twelve. Sarah is seated fairly upright,
her hands clasped in her lap and her posture symmetrical. Jack,
on the other hand, while also leaning back slightly, is much more
asymmetrical with his legs crossed ankle to knee. Jack opens the
discussion. 'Thanks for coming along, Sarah. This is only your
second informal appraisal discussion, so would it help if I re-
capped why I find them useful?'

Although an appraisal discussion can be conducted almost anywhere, choosing neutral territory – especially one where the furniture has no natural 'pole position' – signals that the discussion is between two equals.

'Please,' replies Sarah, still a little uneasy.

'OK. Briefly, there are two reasons. First, I believe we all have a contribution to make to the company and, with the right sort of feedback, we can continuously improve that contribution. Second, I see work as a great source of learning opportunities and, if we look at them the right way, those opportunities can help us develop. So every three months I like to get together to discuss the job, the contribution you are making, any help you need from me, and so on. How does that sound?'

Sarah looks a bit nervous. Jack decides that too much preliminary talk would only make her more uneasy, so he begins the discussion straightaway. He neatly signposts the type of discussion and discloses his motives for having these discussions regularly. He also involves her within seconds *rather than minutes.*

'OK.' Sarah shifts slightly in her seat and, momentarily, her gaze moves down and away.

Sarah is invited to respond but does so with the bare minimum. That, plus her eye movements, signals she is ill at ease . . .

'Normally,' continues Jack, 'I ask team leaders for a brief written review but, as I've been away on this other project, I haven't been able to do so this time. Is there anything particular that you want to discuss?'

'No, not really,' replies Sarah with exactly the same gaze-avoidance.

. . . which happens again very quickly, indicating that her unease is significant.

'In which case, I'll begin,' says Jack, raising his eyebrows.

She indicates that she has no objections, so Jack continues. 'When you became team leader, productivity was good and morale seemed to be very high. I get the impression that, in the last few months, though, things have changed. Is that right?' While he says this his posture remains unchanged, his face relaxed, and his voice pleasant.

So Jack outlines the problem very briefly without being blunt. His use of the assertiveness technique of 'pointing out a discrepancy' also helps him sound non-accusational, something which his body language supports.

'Well,' says Sarah, 'they're not as good as they were initially – but I'm working on it.'

'In what way aren't they as good as they were?' asks Jack, still in his relaxed manner.

Jack probes to learn more.

'I think the clerks resent my promotion,' says Sarah, crossing her arms tightly across her stomach.

Jack holds his chin between his thumb and forefinger and asks Sarah in a calm, gentle voice, 'How do you know?'

Sarah closes her posture, signalling that she is anxious, so Jack signals that he is listening carefully and continues probing.

'They've started to get lazy, to not care. They make mistakes and just don't care about them. They don't check their work like they should and they're taking long lunches, even when there's work to be done.' Sarah is holding herself and crossing her legs even more tightly now, while her shoulders are rising up as if to protect herself even more.

Sarah shows that she is making lots of negative inferences from the clerks' behaviour. And that she is getting even more anxious.

'They're less conscientious and more error-prone than they used to be?' summarises Jack.

'Yes, even though I get on at them and check their work for them, pointing out what they've done wrong.'

Jack repeats what Sarah has said, to show that he is listening and to check his understanding. By paraphrasing he is defusing Sarah's emotive language and helping her stay on his wavelength.

'Despite your efforts, things haven't picked up?' asks Jack.
'No.'

Jack probes . . .

'How do you "get on at them", as you say?'
'Well . . . I just remind them that everything needs to be checked for accuracy,' replies Sarah.
'How, exactly? Give me an example.'

. . . and probes.

Sarah appears to relax a bit. She is now leaning forward, gesticulating. 'Well, if I see someone going to lunch when something is urgent I might say, "I suppose someone will have to skip lunch and do this", but they just ignore me and go to lunch. Or if I find some figures that haven't been checked I might say, "Somebody hasn't been checking their figures. I suppose I'll have to do it." But, again, they just don't care. I've got all this responsibility to see that everything's right and they just don't care. They resent me.' And with that final statement, Sarah resumes her arms-crossed posture.

Sarah is warming to her theme now. Her body language has opened up and she is gesticulating more freely. Jack lets her go on because this is just the information he needs.

Jack sits more upright and says, 'Let me make sure I understand you. When you see something not being done as you think it should, you make a general remark aimed at no one in particular rather than address the person directly. You also feel as if you have sole responsibility for getting things right and, if I understand you

125

correctly, you feel that the rest of the team aren't helping you.'
'Yes, that's about it.'

Again Jack's use of summarising shows that he has listened and that he wants to ensure he has understood.

'And what would you like to achieve?' asks Jack.
'Well . . .' Sarah paused for thought. 'I want them to work like they used to. To care about the job. And . . . I'd also like them to respect me, like they should.'

Having rounded up enough information Jack begins searching for a reason and result that Sarah will find attractive.

'And the approach you've adopted so far hasn't achieved what you want.'
'No,' replies Sarah, looking down.
'Let me ask you a question,' says Jack. Sarah looks up. 'If I had a problem with you and I made oblique references about it, rather than talking to you directly, what thoughts might cross your mind?'
'I suppose I'd wonder why you didn't just speak to me direct.'
'What assumptions might you make about me?'
Sarah thinks a bit more and replies. 'That you were a bit shy, or perhaps a bit distant.'
'And how would you feel?'
'Probably not very good, because you'd be trying to make me feel guilty.' Sarah suddenly looks up. 'Do you think I might have turned the clerks off by not being direct enough with them? I thought it might lead to an argument if I spoke too directly.'

Jack's signposting gets Sarah's attention as well as clarifying his communication. His hypothetical questions also make her think. He will stand a much better chance of changing her behaviour if she thinks it through for herself. He could just tell her what to do but in her current mind-set it is unlikely she would be committed to it.

'It all depends how you do it,' replies Jack. 'Let me summarise. We know what you want to achieve with your team. We also know that the way you're trying to achieve it isn't working. So, let's spend the next few minutes looking at other ways of achieving what you want.'

Jack uses a summary to 'punctuate' this part of the discussion. They are now ready to move on and look at alternatives. It is only a small step to selecting alternatives and coaching Sarah in how to implement the alternative she has chosen.

It would be all too easy to handle this example the wrong way. Most people's natural tendency is to point out to Sarah that, through her behaviour, she is the cause of the problem. All the body language in the early stages of the discussion signals that such an approach would send her further into her shell. Had she appeared more open and confident, a more direct, but still carefully worded, approach might have been satisfactory. Interestingly, had Sarah appeared overly confident the approach Jack adopted would probably still have been the best one in order to make her think it through for herself.

Jack knows he has to tread carefully if he is to get Sarah to 'open up'. He needs to avoid sounding as if he is making an accusation, which he does by tactfully 'pointing out a discrepancy'. He also keeps his body language open and relaxed. His use of probing, reflecting, and summarising help Sarah stay on his wavelength as well as signal that he is listening and is keen to understand. Probing provides very useful information and Jack's use of hypothetical questions helps Sarah think through her behaviours and 'buy into' what she has done more effectively than if she was simply told what she had done. Jack could continue in this way, enabling Sarah to choose her own solution. If it were hers she would be more committed to it than if Jack had simply presented it to her.

Example three

Bill is a 34-year-old scientist working in a research establishment which has recently begun to adopt some commercial practices as it moves closer to privatisation and away from State funding. One of them is that grades relate to jobs rather than to people. The effect is that the only route to promotion is to be transferred into a higher-graded job. Previously anyone who performed satisfactorily could be considered for promotion after specified periods of service, without changing jobs. Ticks in the 'ready for promotion' box on the annual appraisal form for three consecutive years virtually guaranteed promotion. Now a vacancy has to exist, and anyone interested has to compete openly for it via an internal application and selection procedure.

Bill has had five consecutive 'ready for promotion' ticks and has applied for three internal vacancies. Each time he has failed. George has been his manager for six months and has just been informed of Bill's third unsuccessful application. He has to break the news to Bill. George is one of the 'new culture', entrepreneurial scientists and is only one year older than Bill. Bill is very much an academic scientist and has not welcomed the new culture. That, plus his lack of people management skills, accounts for his lack of success in his job applications. Bill's previous boss told him only that he had failed; he made no attempt to find out why.

Owing to the lack of meeting-rooms the conversation is being held in George's office, which is where he normally talks to staff. The office is relatively small and there is nowhere for the two visitors' chairs other than in front of the desk. George has telephoned Bill and asked him to come in. George is already sitting in his own chair behind the desk.

Bill taps on the door and walks straight in. 'You wanted to see me?' He goes straight to one of the visitor's chairs and sits down. He had brought pen and notepaper with him. He looks relaxed, as if he is expecting a conversation about work.

Accepted wisdom is that a desk will form a barrier to hinder discussion. In reality if you always talk to people across your desk and you change that practice only for 'personal' conversations the effect is more likely to be negative than positive.

George looks up and makes eye contact as he smiles. He closes the file he has been looking at. His desk is neat and tidy. What files there are on it are closed and stacked neatly. 'Yes, thanks for coming straight away.' He stops smiling and says, 'George, it's about your recent application for that internal vacancy. It's bad news, I'm afraid. The interview panel have selected someone from G2. I received the memo an hour ago and wanted to let you know as soon as possible.'

George's eye contact and smile gave a warm welcome. The state of his desk signals that he is ready for the conversation and will not be distracted by paperwork. George gets straight to the point, without being blunt. His signposting is quick but effective.

Bill takes in a deep breath and exhales loudly. He stares hard at the bottom of the wall. He knits his eyebrows and his lips tighten. His face pales a little.

The deep breath and the pale face indicate that adrenalin has been released in Bill's body. The eyebrows show anxiety and the lips show that he is holding back what he wants to say.

George says nothing for a while. Then he speaks: 'I've spent the last hour getting hold of a copy of the interview panel's report. Apparently I'm not allowed to give you a copy but I'm happy to let you see it and to discuss the whole thing with you. We can do that now or when you're ready, whichever you prefer.' George's voice was calm and unhurried.

George allows Bill a little recovery time and gives him a choice of continuing or not.

'What's the bloody point?' asks Bill in a resigned tone of voice, still staring at the wall.
'This is the third time an interview panel has turned down your application. What kind of feedback did you get on the other two occasions?' asks George.

Bill's eyes, voice and language form a strong cluster showing how he feels. George treats the question as rhetorical and gently probes.

129

'Absolutely nothing,' replies Bill. Although this time he is looking at George and his body language has otherwise remained the same.

'How did you feel about that?' asks George.

Bill says nothing to begin with. He looks at George, who in turn looks back at him with slightly widened eyes and raised eyebrows while giving a small nod of the head; Bill replies, 'Well, I just thought it was typical. Personnel never do explain why you either got or didn't get promotion.'

Now that Bill has resumed eye contact, George feels he can bring Bill into the conversation more, using a pause to encourage him to talk.

'And how do you feel now?'

'How do you expect me to bloody feel?' retorted Bill with more than a little vexation in his voice.

George holds up his hand towards Bill and nods his head. 'All right, I know, it was a stupid question. But what kinds of thoughts are going through your mind?' George is still calm and relaxed.

Bill clearly was not ready for this question, but George ignores the packaging around his reply and asks the question again, paraphased.

'Well . . .' Bill struggles for words. 'I'm just thinking what the hell have I got to do to get promoted? I get good appraisals. I've been marked ready for promotion for years now and no one can tell me when I'm going to get it. I'm beginning to think that my face doesn't fit or something.'

'What do you know about the criteria for promotion?'

Bill is giving George good-quality information but George does not respond to it directly. Instead he asks Bill a question designed to get him thinking. Responding directly would be easy but it would also push the conversation towards either 'verbal ping-pong' or a defend/attack spiral.

'Presumably you've got to be good at your job. That's the way it always used to work. Well, I am good at my job. Look at my appraisals.' Bill is now facing George directly, sitting bolt upright in his chair with both feet firmly on the ground. The comment about his appraisal is accompanied by two open palms, fingers down, in George's direction.

Bill's body language is now more open but it is a combination of standing his ground and pleading with George for help, as if he is torn between two emotions. It is also likely that he is still working on beliefs *relevant to the 'old culture' rather than the 'new culture'.*

'Those aren't the current criteria,' replies George. 'It's now based entirely on fulfilling the criteria for the job for which you are applying. What do you know about most of the jobs at the grade above yours?'

Bill exhales loudly again and says, 'Well, I suppose you've got to be good at managing people and be a bit commercial. But I've been doing my job well for years. Doesn't that count for anything?'

This is a logical question from George but Bill's loud sigh indicates that he is unhappy with the topic.

'Only if it's related to the job for which you're applying. Would you like to see what the interview panel said about you?'
'OK.'

George responds to Bill's remark but avoids the temptation to leave it there by moving the conversation on.

George hands Bill the file from his desk and waits while Bill reads the report. Eventually he asks, 'How do you feel about what they've said?'

'Well, I'm pleased to see that they recognised my past performance and my technical ability,' replies Bill grudgingly.

'What does it say you need more of?'

'Just like I was saying,' says Bill. 'More commercial awareness and people management experience. But so what?' Bill becomes

131

louder now. 'Even if I get those things, can you tell me when I'll
get promoted?' Bill is staring hard into George's eyes and leaning forward over the desk.

*Bill's body language shows that his temper is beginning to
rise but, again . . .*

George retains his composure and says calmly, 'Bill, no one
can tell you that. It all depends on vacancies.' Bill leans back in
his chair, crossing his legs tightly knee to knee and his arms
tightly across his body. He also swivels away slightly from
George. George continues: 'But if you know what you need to
do to give yourself a decent chance of promotion, and if you
want promotion, we can work out a plan to get you the necessary
experience.'

*George ignores the packaging and stays in control of his
own behaviour, even when Bill shows that he is opting out
of the conversation.*

'What do you mean, "If I *want* promotion"?' asks Bill sarcas-
tically, still in his turned-away posture.
'Not everyone does,' replies George. 'Sure, most people
would welcome the extra money but they don't all welcome the
extra responsibility or the roles.'
'How do you mean?' asks Bill, turning more towards George.
'Well, how would you feel if you had to spend more time on
administration than research, if you had to make decisions about
budgets, or had to spend more time with your staff than with
your test-tubes?'

*George knows that Bill needs to think things through
rather than be told them, so he makes even this statement
a question.*

'Oh I see what you mean,' replies Bill quietly.
'What you and I can do is talk through issues like that. I can't
make up your mind for you but I can help you see the wood for
the trees. If you do want to go for promotion again, I can also
help you get some of the experience you'll need. What I can't do

is motivate you.' And here George leans forward slightly, looks Bill directly in the eye, and lowers his voice: 'That has to come from inside you.'

George sees that Bill is more receptive and so feels it is OK to make a statement rather than phrase what he wants to say as a question.

Bill is now more relaxed although very pensive. 'So what do you think I should do now?' he asks quietly.

'Recognise that you're only human and that you've received some bad news. Don't feel awkward about being disappointed. And don't blame either yourself or the organisation. Times are changing and it takes time to adjust. Think of what you want out of the job and think of what you feel comfortable or uncomfortable doing. In the meantime, I'm sorry you didn't get the job but', he smiles, 'I'm glad I won't be losing you . . . not just yet, anyway.'

He also points to the need to be tolerant.

Thankfully there are not many people who enjoy giving bad news. For most of us it is an unpleasant experience. The prospect of it is enough to start the fight-or-flight response in most of us. Some people will therefore psyche themselves up and go in too bluntly, almost as if they are protecting themselves from the other person with a barrier impervious to emotions or even empathy. Other people will put off the moment of delivering the bad news, even if only for a few seconds, by rambling around the point. The effect of both approaches is rarely positive. It is far better briefly to signpost, to get the other person onto your wavelength, and then to give them the bad news straight. That means being concise, accurate and not using emotive words. 'The interview panel have selected someone from G2' means, of course, the same as 'You've failed yet again.' It is just a lot less emotive.

Another point at this stage regards George's desk. Some people may disagree but a desk is not automatically a barrier. Had George left papers and open files on it the potential for distraction might then have made it a barrier. Had George used it as a status symbol and exaggerated his importance whilst behind it (remember the 'top dog' posture?) it would have been a barrier. Countless people on courses have told me that if their boss uncharacteristically sits on the same side of the desk as they are, they assume he has just been on an interpersonal skills course!

Bill's body language is very strong. It shows that he is upset. Consequently George makes an allowance for the fact that Bill's emotions have been triggered and that he is unlikely to choose his words carefully, and may even take out his frustration on George. People who receive bad news behave that way. They may be upset with the message but they may still vent their emotions on the messenger. George asks Bill questions to help with that venting process. He also looks as if he has as long to discuss it as Bill may need for him to listen.

Something else to watch for when the other person reacts to bad news is defending yourself against their attacks. They may criticise the company, the decision-makers, the decision, and even you. It is natural to want to defend yourself. But the purpose of their attack is to make themselves feel better, not to engage in a rational debate. Defend too hard and you can find yourself in a defend/attack spiral.

Summary

Jane, Jack and George are all careful to move at the other person's pace. They could, no doubt, get the discussions over much more quickly than they did but without the same effect. They use lots of signposting, summarising, and checking to ensure that they and the other person stay on the same wavelength.

All three conversations are characterised by lots of involvement from the other person. Look at the ratios of talking. While it is the other person who does the most of the talking it is Jane, Jack and George who are in control of the pace and direction of the discussion. They use a lot of probing and listening. The probing is mostly open with a lot of hypothetical questions. Much of it is designed to make the other person think things through for themselves as well as to uncover relevant information. It might be quicker just to tell them, but not nearly so effective.

They make no attempt to manipulate the other person and even manage to avoid being manipulated on more than one occasion.

They utilise assertive thinking and behaviours to stand up for themselves and to side-step attempted manipulation from the other person. Yet they remember that the other person is only human and may react in unproductive ways. At no time, however, do they abdicate responsibility for their thoughts and actions. They behave by design rather than by default.

They use the information they uncover to persuade the other person by presenting their ideas in terms the other person will appreciate. Furthermore they deliberately adopt behaviours that are likely to trigger productive responses from the other person and they carefully avoid the no-noes and 'wild card' behaviours.

They carefully manage their own body language so that it supports what they want to achieve and they observe with equal care the other person's, modifying their approach in response to negative and positive signals.

In short they use their behaviour as the tool that will help deliver the outcome they want to achieve, rather than let it take care of itself. In doing so, they know that there is no guarantee the other person will react in the 'textbook' manner and that it is therefore possible they may not get what they want. But Jane, Jack and George do know that adopting the right, principled and productive behaviours themselves will give them the best possible chance of success.

5

Gameplans

Introduction

Here is an analogy: within reason, a cook could use a cupboard-full of ingredients to produce a variety of different meals by using them in different quantities and cooking them in different ways. So we can use our core skills for a variety of different situations by using them in different quantities and in different ways. This chapter shows how to do that by presenting a selection of 'gameplans' aimed at a variety of situations that people sometimes find difficult.

A 'gameplan' is a set of tactics or the 'strategy' that can be adopted for a given situation. The situations covered will include those that people on my courses refer to as the most common or most troublesome. They are:

- appraisals – giving feedback on performance
- praising someone for something they have done, to encourage more of the same
- reprimanding and giving constructive criticism, to discourage negative behaviour
- counselling to resolve a personal problem
- giving bad news to someone
- coaching to improve performance
- handling people who cause you delays
- negotiating
- resolving a difference of opinion
- persuading someone to use your services
- leading a productive meeting
- selecting the right candidate.

For each situation I will describe the main issues and problems and conclude with a gameplan designed for easy reference. As the nature of each situation varies so does each of the following sections. Some are more prescriptive than others and some are more detailed than others. Their general format, however, is the same. You can use the gameplans to improve your general knowledge of influencing skills or as a source of reference. You may for example want to home in on situations you have always found difficult in the past so that you can handle them better if they arise in the future. Or you may want to focus on situations that you have not come across before. Or you may want to prepare for a particularly tricky discussion you know will happen soon.

Appraisals – giving feedback on performance

Introduction

Organisations in all sectors are becoming ever more performance-conscious. At a time of writing (1994) there is a lot of debate in the health service about whether clinical staff could or should be given personal job-objectives. A key activity in the process of performance management is the conversation between boss and subordinate (or however the relationship is described) during which the boss discusses performance with the subordinate in an attempt to improve performance in the future.

While subordinates are often on the receiving end of feedback on their performance it is rarely quality feedback. Far too many managers only give feedback when they need to (that is, when they spot a problem or, less frequently, when they see something good happening). Feedback is therefore more likely to be negative than positive. Consequently it is usually an uncomfortable experience for both manager and subordinate.

Sometimes it happens so infrequently that the whole process is taken over by another department (usually that of personnel) who develop special documentation and systems to turn it into an annual event. As a consequence they become the police officers of the procedures and the custodians of the completed forms. Appraisal tends to happen, therefore, far too infrequently and its effectiveness can diminish to such an extent that it is not recognised as a productive management activity. The relationship between boss and subordinate (and performance) is the poorer for it.

Yet such is the focus on performance in most organisations, and the power of feedback so great, that the process of giving feedback deserves significant attention from all managers.

Problems

Here are the main problems with the process of giving feedback:

- *There is unclear focus.* It is usually the boss who initiates the discussion and it is understandably seen as his or her meeting. Sometimes it is even referred to as an 'interview'! The purpose is rarely clear. (In my experience few people actually see such a discussion as the prime means of improving performance.) Sometimes managers know the performance they want improved (and hence the behaviour they want the subordinate to change) but confuse the issue by talking about the subordinate's personality or attitude. The sudden bout of lateness is discussed as 'your deteriorating motivation'; the customer complaint is discussed as 'your poor attitude towards customers'.
- *Open discussion is hampered by the hierarchical relationship between the two participants.* Managers see it as their role to 'take charge' of the discussion and subordinates feel threatened and defensive. Attempts to put subordinates at ease often backfire because they revolve around two minutes' idle chat about something irrelevant such as the weather (which only serves to heighten subordinates' anxiety as they wonder why their boss is talking about something so irrelevant – 'The feedback must be bad if the boss has to soften me up this much'!).
- *Managers can feel uncomfortable about giving feedback to staff, especially where performance has been under par.* They can worry about what it will do to their working relationship with the subordinate, or about whether they have the credibility to carry it through.

  In the first case they dilute the criticism by minimising the message. Poor performance becomes 'a little bit disappointing' or 'not quite as good as I would have hoped'. It is treated therefore as of little importance. In the second case they boost their own morale by exaggerating the problem. Under-par performance becomes 'wholly unacceptable' or 'thoroughly disappointing'. The subordinate remembers more about the unjust way they have been treated rather than the behaviour changes the boss wants to encourage.

- *Managers tend to talk too much and listen too little.* Whether through fear of losing control or a desire to 'lead the discussion' is difficult to say, but the result is that subordinates rarely feel as if their views have been given sufficient hearing, and they do not 'buy into' the same conclusions as the managers.

To overcome these problems and gain the benefits of giving feedback regularly to staff on their performance the following gameplan will help.

1 Prepare

- Facilitate preparation by your staff and brief them clearly on the purpose of the discussion (namely, to improve working relationships and performance, not to tell them what the company thinks of them). Ensure they know they will be involved in the discussion as a participant, not as a recipient of information from you. Foster the thinking pattern that *they* are responsible for their performance, albeit with help from you.
- Prepare yourself. What were the key results or performance standards you agreed or expected? How has actual performance compared? What are the relevant behaviours you notice (as opposed to personality traits you assume)? Are your beliefs in order? You have a right to expect performance of a certain standard and to give feedback on performance. Your subordinate also has a right to be listened to, be treated fairly, and feel good about the discussion.
- Prepare the location. You need an environment where you will both be relaxed and feel alright about speaking frankly. That may require 'neutral' territory such as a meeting-room.

2 Get the opening right

In just the same way that you only have one chance to make a first impression the opening is your major signposting/focusing opportunity, so do not waste it. Impressions created in the first few seconds of the discussion will set up your subordinate's thinking patterns for the rest of it.

Conversations about the weather, traffic conditions, and families are productive only if relevant. (If your subordinate has driven for two hours to get there a conversation about the journey will be relevant; if you have spoken to him or her earlier that day already, it will not.) Better to explain the purpose of the discussion and how you would like to go about it and ask if they feel OK about that. (This also serves to involve them within the first 15 seconds, which is what you should aim to do.)

3 Get the style right

Try adopting the following sequence for every 'section' of the discussion:

- Signpost – ie what you want to talk about and why.
- Use a question to encourage the subordinate to begin thinking and talking; continue that process by probing.
- Use your body language and tone of voice to stay neutral and relaxed, but attentive. Above all, avoid sounding like an interrogator or someone whose mind is already made up.
- Check your understanding of what they are saying, especially about concerns they have.
- Summarise what you have covered/agreed etc.

Generally, a good discussion of this sort is characterised by the boss listening at least twice as much as he or she speaks, and probably more. You will therefore need to display a lot of listening behaviours to encourage your subordinate to talk. You will need to remember that probing, reflecting, and summarising are essential parts of active listening. The aim, remember, is to improve the subordinate's performance, so it helps if all the solutions are theirs. So you will need to use questions to encourage them to rethink their views.

If the appraisal is a productive one it is likely that you will need to speak frankly. To avoid the danger of triggering off an inappropriate reaction in the subordinate, pay special attention to avoiding emotive terminology and to maintaining a neutral tone of voice – but maintain the impact of what you are saying with direct eye contact.

4 Close effectively

Conclude the discussion with a summary of specific action. Merely agreeing to 'do something about . . .', or 'try to do better', or go on such and such a course 'some time soon' is the road to mediocrity. Be specific. Say, for example: 'So, I'm going to attend three sales meetings with you over the next two weeks from the list you supply tomorrow. I'll observe how you handle negotiations, without intervening, and then we'll be able to see how we can get these margins back up to target. Is that your understanding?'

A nice, and time-saving, touch if the discussion has been a long one is to ask the subordinate to produce a written summary within 24 hours. Handwritten will usually suffice. It has the effect of reassuring them that theirs is the version to be recorded.

5 Consider the following 'dos and don'ts'

Do:

- treat the other person as an equal party to the conversation, whatever your respective positions in the hierarchy
- be specific, whether you are talking about quantifiable results or reported behaviours
- pay attention to successes, particularly how behaviours from a successful area can be transferred to a less successful area.

Don't:

- use 'red rag' words and phrases such as, 'I've called you in to discuss . . .' Headteachers *call in* their pupils; managers *ask to see* their subordinates.
- describe performance as 'satisfactory' or 'average'. Only underperformers like to be described thus; to everyone else it is a derogatory description, even if it is statistically accurate.
- hide behind the 'corporate we'; the relationship in focus is between you and your subordinate, not them and the organisation.

141

Conclusion

On the whole, managers do not give enough feedback of the right quality to their staff. This is a pity because constructive feedback is not only a significant motivator: it is also the most cost-effective route to improved performance. Managers shy away from it for a variety of reasons: it is not recognised as being a productive use of time; it is too uncomfortable; or they do not see the need, because 'we talk every day, don't we?' When feedback is given it is easy to make it too general, too negative, too antagonistic, or too one-sided, and then not to follow up the discussion.

The gameplan outlined here shows you how to capitalise on the process and enhance your own credibility as a boss.

Table 5.1
Appraisals – giving feedback on performance

1 Prepare	• Look at the work tasks, objectives, problems etc. • Keep records; do not rely on memory. • Encourage staff member to prepare.
2 Get the opening night	• Minimal small talk. • Outline the format of the discussion. • Involve staff member within first few seconds. • Use body language to set tone of discussion.
3 Get the style right	• Focus on behaviour, not personality or attitude. • Be direct, accurate and concise; avoid emotive language; be assertive. • Probe and reflect to encourage staff member to think. • Listen at least 60 per cent of time.
4 Close effectively	• What will staff member do to improve performance? Agree specifics. • Summarise.

Praising

Introduction

Over the years, I have read many companies' annual report and accounts – not for the financial statements, but for the information contained in the chairman's statement. It is a useful start to getting to know a company. The statement contains a concise review of the year and a preview of future plans and priorities. I have noticed that they almost always contain 'a big thank-you to all our staff – our most valuable asset'. Sometimes I think to myself, 'Then why do your customers think of them as your biggest liability?'

It is now over a decade since Tom Peters' and Robert Waterman's *In Search of Excellence* (New York, Harper Row, 1982) turned the spotlight on the relationship between people and performance. Consider the following points:

- Much of what constitutes good performance today is determined by employees' attitudes.
- Attitudes are influenced by a variety of factors from the formal pay and conditions to the informal 'connection' between employees and the tasks they perform (that is, whether they feel good about their work or whether they feel alienated from it).
- While we are basically psychological animals, and our behaviour can be conditioned using appropriate rewards and punishments, we tend to perform better when we *want* to perform rather than when we feel we are *coerced* into performing.
- Effective praising, while insufficient on its own, is an essential element in establishing and maintaining the desire to perform well.

As good performance is something we all want from our staff and colleagues it makes sense to use our behaviour to link our intentions to the results we want.

Praise makes us feel more secure and more valued. It makes us feel better about ourselves and it strengthens relationships. We like these feelings and so do more of what earns the praise, even if the praise happens only intermittently.

Problems

Praising, however, is beset with problems:

- *It does not come naturally to most people, especially managers.* When Charles Margerison conducted research into managerial influencing styles he identified four categories – 'Rewards and Punishments', 'Participation & Trust', 'Common Vision' and 'Assertive Persuasion' (which I prefer to call 'Aggressive Persuasion' as it involves very little listening). He noted that the commonest style for managers, especially British ones, is 'Rewards and Punishments', with the punishment more evident than the reward!

  The reason praising does not come naturally to most people is probably because our attention is drawn more readily to deviations than to norms, and the deviations we are primed to seek out are those that will cause us problems. In other words we find it easier to catch people doing something wrong than doing something right!
- *When we do catch people doing something right, we are prone to* **contaminate** *the praise we give them.* We can demonstrate insincerity by paying insufficient attention to the other person, – for example, by congratulating them on something while we search in the drawer for a missing file. There is minimal eye contact, they know our concentration is elsewhere, and the matter is treated fleetingly. We can turn the praise into a criticism: 'That was good. What a pity you can't do that more often'; or, 'You handled that supplier very well. I wish you were as thorough with your own staff.' We can turn it into bribery by mentioning it when we want something, so that it appears conditional. 'I was very impressed with the way you handled that supplier. I was wondering, would you mind preparing these figures for me?' Finally we can minimise it by being too reserved about it. 'I saw the way you handled that supplier. It was *quite* good.' (I have tested that sentence on hundreds of people. They all feel that the word 'quite' detracts dramatically from the word 'good'.) Contaminated praise either has very little, or a negative, effect.

To overcome these problems and gain the benefits of praising staff the following gameplan will help.

1 Praise quickly

The old saying 'strike while the iron is hot' is very apt. In praising, you are attempting to shape someone's behaviour and the praising will have most effect close to the actual event concerned. So praise as soon as possible after the event or, at least, as soon as you hear about it.

An exception to this rule might be something like a 'salesperson of the month' award or a 'team player of the quarter' celebration. But they would be the exception. Saving up praise for, say, the quarterly appraisal will not shape behaviour very well.

2 Specify what

You are praising because you want the other person to do more of the same, as it were, so you need to be sure they understand what 'more of the same' actually is. You need to be precise, therefore, in your terminology. 'That was good' is unlikely to be accurate enough whereas the following comment is much more precise: 'The way you stayed calm while that customer was ranting and raving was really impressive – and then you used that questioning technique to calm him down and get to the bottom of his complaint. That was good.'

It will help if you are clear in your own mind about exactly what you want to encourage in others. It is effort, dedication, commitment, responsiveness, teamwork, appearance, tidiness, openness, safety, risk-taking, or what? As a rule keep it close to the mission, values, attitudes, actions etc you are trying to encourage generally, because praising is one of the ways managers 'walk the talk'.

3 Give it impact

You want the other person to feel good about the experience of being praised; you want to trigger their positive emotions. So:

- After describing the behaviour you are praising, state how *you* feel about it. This bit of self-disclosure may sound odd but it adds to the sincerity.

145

- Pause for a few seconds to let your remarks sink in.
- Maintain eye contact throughout.
- Smile, look pleased, look relaxed.

4 Milk it, but don't overegg it!

The results of effective praising can be so positive that it is worth squeezing the maximum benefit from it. There are two positive ways in which you can 'milk' a praising. First, probe. Ask the other person some questions about what they accomplished and how they went about it. 'What went through your mind when the customer came in?'; 'How did you manage to stay so calm?'; or 'How long did it take you to learn that?' Your purpose is to demonstrate interest, so the questions need to be genuine and the topic needs to be overtly worth the effort. Done correctly, this is a good positive and unconditional pat on the back.

Second, if the behaviour you are praising is significant enough discuss what the other person learnt and see how that learning can be transferred to other aspects of their job. Say, for example, 'The questioning technique you used to help calm down that customer really worked well. How can you use that approach when Big John in dispatch loses his temper?' In this way your praising becomes a mini coaching session.

There is a note of caution to sound, however. Praising can shape people's behaviour most effectively when it is intermittent. Praise too frequently, or praise trivial events, and you will devalue both the effect and your own credibility.

5 Close neatly

Again, with eye contact and a smile, encourage your subordinates to deliver more of the same.

Conclusion

So you can use praise with your staff, your colleagues, your manager, and so on to encourage more of the behaviour you want from them. Yes, you can praise your boss! I do not mean underhand, favour-seeking praise such as, 'Gee, boss, you really handled the chief executive well then. You're so smart!' But let's say that your boss has a habit of delegating tasks to you without telling you their relative priorities (sound familiar?). And let's say that one day you persevere and get him or her to suggest priorities. You could say, 'Thanks, it helps to know what needs to be done first. I feel more confident that I'll be working on the right things now. I appreciate it when you spend a minute explaining priorities like that. Thank you.' And you accompany these words with the right eye contact, the right tone of voice, the right facial expression and, of course, the little pause for impact. You will stand a good chance of getting the priorities explained without asking next time.

Praising works in incremental steps. You are encouraging someone to move in the direction you want, so you do not have to wait until they are performing perfectly before you praise them. I remember a bank manager telling me about a young clerk who worked in his branch. (Let's call the clerk Michael.) Michael was exceptionally untidy. His desk and his drawers were a mess. He mislaid papers, allowed documents from one file to get caught in the paper clips of documents from other files, and so on. The bank manager had done everything he could think of to cure Michael of his untidiness. He had shown him how to set up systems, counselled him in private, yelled at him in public, formally disciplined him, and so on. The consequent improvements did not last and it was not long before Michael's desk was its usual chaos.

One day Michael came in late and had not had time to wreak his usual havoc when the manager passed his desk. This time the manager remembered my advice on praising, and so praised Michael for his tidy desk (even though he knew it was only accidentally tidy). It must have had the right impact because the next time I saw the manager he told me that Michael's desk, while it would win no prizes, was much tidier than it had ever been in the past – and it stayed that way.

Conclusion

Performance tends to be affected by how we feel about the tasks we carry out. We can affect how people feel about their work and encourage them to perform in certain ways by praising them. If we praise the wrong way, the effect can be negative. If we praise the right way, however, the effects tend to be very positive.

Table 5.2
Praising

1 Praise quickly	• The closer to the event, the greater the impact of praising will be.
2 Specify what	• Be precise and descriptive.
3 Give it impact	• Provide impact by: – probing – self-disclosure with a pause, eye contact, and a smile. • See what aspects of behaviour can transfer to other tasks.
4 Milk it, but don't overegg it	• Do not overdo it. • Probe, to show interest. • Draw out lessons for the future from present success.
5 Close neatly	• Repeat the aspect you are praising. • Smile, with eye contact. • Thank the other person.

Reprimanding and giving constructive criticism

Introduction

One of the most refreshing things to happen in the world of work in the last 15 years has been the emergence of non-academic, easy-to-read books on management. One that justifiably took the world by storm in the early 1980s was *The One Minute Manager* (London, Fontana, 1983) by Kenneth Blanchard and Spencer Johnson. This book and its companion volume, *Putting the One Minute Manager to Work* (London, Fontana/Collins, 1984) by Kenneth Blanchard and Robert Lorber, had two very simple, but powerful, messages for managers. The first was that if you want your staff to be high-achievers you have to set clear goals with them and then help them progress in the right direction by giving praise when you see them performing well, and reprimanding when you see them performing negligently. As I mentioned in the last section, most of us do not capitalise on praising as much as we could; we have a predisposition to catching people doing something wrong rather than something right. The second message of these two books was that, to be effective, you have to praise and reprimand in a certain way.

In the last section I covered praising, and amended and added to the Blanchard et al. recommendations according to what my course participants have told me passes the 'TSR Test' (see page viii). In this section I want to do the same with reprimanding.

I should state at the beginning that I have coupled it with giving constructive criticism, because I see the two as being very similar. Both share a common aim in that we are trying to get someone to change their behaviour for the better. They can differ in that a reprimand could be formal or informal. In uniformed occupations, particularly, such as the police force or the fire service, a formal reprimand would be conducted in a way that few of us would tolerate in a non-uniformed occupation. So I shall comment on such formal reprimands by way of additional notes to the gameplan that follows.

Problems

Reprimanding and criticising are beset with more problems than praising:

- *Most of us enjoy praise, but few enjoy reprimands or criticism.* Those who do enjoy the latter are either enthusiastic masochists or are suffering from very low self-esteem. (Strange though it may seem, in such cases the criticism provides a 'pay-off' by confirming their view of themselves and thereby relieving them of the need to try to improve. After all, if someone receives confirmation that they really are useless at something there is no point in 'attempting the impossible', so they can safely stay as they are. Even though they may not like themselves as they are it is preferable to the risk of attempting to change. Should you feel that way at times a good book on assertiveness might help.)

For most of us, criticism just hits the playback button on childhood 'tapes', and unpleasant feelings emerge. Let me explain. Do you remember what I was saying, on the subject of assertiveness, about children living in a land dominated by giants and rules? Transgressing a rule usually brings swift criticism or reprimand from one of the giants. There are two points to make here. First, not many of the giants know how to reprimand or criticise effectively: they usually fail to differentiate between the behaviour they want altered and the person exhibiting the behaviour. In other words, it is *we* who are being criticised, not our *behaviour*. This creates very negative feelings within us. Second, the rules are usually very one-sided in that they are specified from the giants' viewpoints, not the children's. So in effect we are often told off for being five years old rather than twenty-five years old; for being naturally fun-loving rather than being naturally serious; for not being as dexterous as an adult, and so on. Consequently the negative feelings grow stronger. We feel unjustly treated, resentful, angry, ashamed etc, etc. All these feelings are recorded, ready to be replayed in adulthood as soon as someone hits the playback button. Their effect is to make us less susceptible to change our behaviour positively as a result of being reprimanded or criticised.

- *When reprimanding or criticising we can hit the other person's playback button in two main ways.* They both stem from the fact that not many of us enjoy criticising. (If you do, you are probably either a sadist, in which case you might be happier working as a mercenary or as a vivisectionist, or you have a high *critical parent* – see below.) And here we need to go off at a tangent!

According to well-respected theories of transactional analysis we all have three aspects to our mental make-up. One contains all the 'rules of the road' for life that we acquired from authority figures around us, usually our parents. Accordingly this aspect is known as *the parent*. Another aspect of our mental make-up contains the characteristics we associate with childhood such as loving fun, creativity, spontaneity, emotions, and so on. Accordingly this aspect is known as *the child.* The last aspect of our mental make-up is the rational, analytical, unemotional, problem-solving bit which is labelled *the adult.* In grown-ups who are well-balanced these three aspects of mental make-up are equal and can be engaged at will, whenever relevant.

Unfortunately, for many of us, these aspects can be well and truly out of balance. It is possible to have *a dominant child,* which would make someone a bit irresponsible, irrational, unpredictable, emotional, and manipulative. It is possible to have *a dominant adult,* which would make someone rather cold, unemotional, uncaring, and insensitive to others. It is also possible to have *a dominant parent.* This can on the one hand make people excessively nurturing (a real 'mother hen') or on the other excessively critical as a result of the quantity and intensity of the 'rules' they carry around in their heads about 'the way things should be'. They see only two ways of doing anything – their way and the wrong way! Hence they are into criticism in a big way, not for the satisfaction of the sadist but out of a genuine desire to have things done in what they regard as 'the proper way'. (End of tangent.)

Whether we have a high critical parent or just enjoy finding fault we often adopt one of two stances when criticising, in order to make ourselves more comfortable. The first is to psyche ourselves up and go in too hard. This is usually characterised by *exaggeration.* 'You've been late twice this week' becomes 'I'm fed up with the way you're always coming in late these days.' A '10 per cent shortfall' becomes 'a wholly disgraceful performance'. It is as if we boost our case, and hence our confidence, by this exaggeration and generalisation. The second stance is to *minimise* the problem, in order to lessen the likelihood of confrontation. 'You've been late twice this week' becomes 'I hope you don't mind my mentioning it, but . . . er . . . your time-keeping isn't . . . er . . . quite as good as it . . . um . . . used to be.' The '10 per cent shortfall' becomes 'just a teeny little bit off-target'.

The effect is that the other person remembers more about the packaging than the message and as a result our attempt at altering their behaviour is much less effective.

- *This 'packaging not the message' problem reoccurs when we forget to focus on behaviour and allow ourselves to make assumptions.* Instead of discussing the behaviour to be changed we try to discuss attitudes and personality traits. Consequently we are not only in the realms of guesswork but are also criticising the person rather than their behaviour, which is likely to make them overly defensive.

- *The final problem is inconsistency.* Most of us are more likely to criticise and reprimand when our emotions are running high than when we are feeling OK. If we have just been hauled over the coals by our boss we feel like doing something similar to someone else. If we are on edge we become likely to snap. If we are very nervous about a piece of work, we are likely to make a meal out of errors that we might otherwise not even notice. While we are all human, and prone to human emotions, the problem with inconsistency is that it devalues the effectiveness of our attempts to alter someone's behaviour, because the act of reprimanding or criticising loses credibility.

It will help, therefore, if you follow the next gameplan.

1 Reprimand or criticise quickly

As with praising, the further away from the event, the smaller will be the impact of a reprimand or criticism. So act as soon as possible after the event, or as soon as you hear about it – with an important proviso! If the event, whatever it is, has caused your emotions to run very high consider delaying the reprimand or criticism until you have calmed down. That way you will be more rational and less prone to exaggerate, use emotive language, make assumptions, and so on.

2 Specify what

You are reprimanding or criticising because you want the other person to do less of something, so you need to be sure that they understand what that 'something' actually is. You need to be precise, therefore, in your terminology. As with praising, it will help if you are clear in your own mind about exactly what behaviour you want to discourage in others. Is it laziness, lack of effort of commitment, slow responsiveness, not supporting the team, sloppy appearance, untidiness, not sharing information, playing safe all the time, or what? Again, keep it close to the mission, values, attitudes, actions etc you are trying to encourage generally, because this is another of the ways managers 'walk the talk' – hence my comments earlier on consistency.

One way you can be specific, ensure that you focus on behaviour, and keep your own emotions in check is to use the assertiveness technique of *pointing out a discrepancy*. Returning to time-keeping example above you might say, 'You've always been a good time-keeper but you've been late twice this week. Why is that?' Pointing out a discrepancy works equally well in more serious situations, for example: 'To complete this project on time I have had to enlist the resources of a variety of departments. Every departmental head has helped, even at great personal inconvenience, except for you. Why is that?'

It has the effect of being descriptive and non-accusatory; it also immediately involves the other person, making them less emotionally defensive. They still defend themselves but they will do so more openly and rationally.

3 Check you've got it right

Even if you are 100 per cent certain of your facts, still check that you have got it right, for example: 'Everyone else is going to work late to get this order out in time but you aren't. Is that correct?; or 'I've just heard you using a lot of bad language in the office. Am I right?' The reason for checking is twofold. First, there may just be a slight chance that you have not got the full picture.

I once read about an employee who punched a customer. The customer complained and had independent witnesses. The employee was summarily dismissed. It later emerged that the customer had first head-butted the employee and was about to do so again. No one saw that first attack. So what appeared to be an unprovoked attack was really self-defence. Thankfully not all cases are this extreme but you need to check. If the other person has genuine information that alters the situation then thank them for it and stop there. Do not press on through fear of losing face. You will lose infinitely more face by carrying on.

Second, checking that you have got it right shows that, by allowing the other person to present their side, you are not jumping to conclusions. This adds to your credibility and the impact of the discussion.

When the other person is responding, you need to show that you are listening with eye contact, head nods, reflecting, and summaries to check understanding.

When a reprimand is official, especially in uniformed occupations, you may find it appropriate to add to the formality of the occasion. The easiest way is to adopt a formal seating-arrangement, with the participants sitting opposite each other across a table or desk, and to sit formally (like a newsreader, upright, slightly forward, with hands clasped on the table in front of you). I have heard that in uniformed occupations the 'atmosphere' would be enhanced by keeping the 'defendant' standing. This knowledge makes me, personally, feel very uncomfortable because it sounds old-fashioned and counter-productive.

You should also be aware that the more formal the situation, the more your organisation's procedures will become relevant. The other person may have the right to a certain amount of notice of the discussion, to be accompanied by a colleague or union representative, and to recourse to a higher authority if they disagree with you. You will probably also have to produce a written record of the discussion.

The aim, I would suggest, is to use reprimanding and criticising as positively as possible so that the formal situations become an infrequent last resort.

4 Give it some positive impact

To be effective the reprimand or criticism must have positive rather than negative impact. Negative impact will result from a variety of causes. For example reprimanding or criticising in public makes people feel very awkward and they will either clam up or counter-attack. Either way your attempt to alter their behaviour will prove less effective than it might otherwise be.

You need to be concise without being blunt. The more you ramble, the less accurate you are. Pointing out a discrepancy helps here too. Self-disclosure, stating how the event has made you feel (again accurately, without exaggeration), adds to the impact.

Your posture needs to be upright, open, and relaxed. If you

feel anxious about the encounter, you may well 'close up' by crossing your legs tightly, 'shrinking' a little, protecting your abdomen, averting your eyes, and covering your mouth with your hand. If you feel angry about the event, this will show itself in a 'full-frontal' posture (head, torso and feet all facing the other person), an expansive chest, attacking gestures such as finger-wagging or finger-jabbing, and a tight-lipped facial expression with lowered eyebrows and excessive eye contact. Your tone of voice needs to be neutral rather than shaky or stern, your eye contact direct and relatively constant, but without the lowered eyebrows and tight lips of the angry person.

You might have to persist, rather than be fobbed off, by using the 'broken record' to make your point. You will have to let the other person know what the consequences will be if they do not change their behaviour as you have described. Here, you will need to pay special attention to your tone of voice. You want what you are saying to be received as a straightforward statement of cause and effect, not as a threat.

5 End on a high note

Remember, the other person must be left in no doubt what you want them to do differently, so repeat it. Also, you want them to remember the message, not the packaging, so remind them that your concern is with what has happened, not with them.

This applies whether the person you are criticising is a member of your staff, someone else's staff, a colleague, your child, your spouse, or your next-door neighbour. You are speaking up for what you want and trying to get the other person to agree with you. The more positively you handle the discussion, the better they will feel about it and the better your chance of success. To do that your focus needs to be on the behaviour, your attention on the person, and your effort on the relationship.

Conclusion

As a manager, you have both a right and a duty to give feedback on performance. As a colleague, subordinate, customer etc, you have a right to ask other people to change. Reprimanding and criticising trigger so many emotions in both the people involved that when you do it effectively you are not only more likely to achieve what you want but you will also be improving your credibility.

Table 5.3

Reprimanding and giving constructive criticism

1 Reprimand or criticise	• – unless emotions are running very high.
2 Specify what	• Be accurate: – no exaggeration – no minimalisation – no assumptions about personality or motives. • No emotive language; point out a discrepancy. • Pay attention to your eye contact, posture and tone of voice.
3 Check you've got it right	• Listen.
4 Give it some positive impact	• Pause, with eye contact. • If necessary, use the 'broken record' and point out the consequence of not changing.
5 End on a high note	• Focus on behaviour. • Sound and look positive.

Counselling to resolve a personal problem

Introduction

You can become involved in a counselling discussion for one of two reasons. Someone can approach you and ask for help, or you can spot something that concerns you and so *you* approach *them* and offer help. Serious counselling discussions, say, where someone is suffering from clinical depression, are best left to experts, but everyday situations should be within the range of most people trained in influencing skills.

But what is counselling? Let's begin by looking at what it is not. It is not coaching someone to improve their knowledge or skills. Neither is it reprimanding or criticising someone to let them know how their behaviour has differed from requirements, and what will happen if they do not change it. It is where someone has a problem, often of a personal nature, for which they, and only they, have to find the wherewithal to solve. Such problems can range from domestic troubles and money worries to negative attitudes towards a new organisation structure or a personality clash with other people. You are not only looking for a solution, therefore: you are trying to stimulate the motivation to do something about it.

The need to counsel people with regard to personal problems is often related to stress, and stress itself often appears during times of change, especially unwelcome change. Many of the people participating in my courses (on almost any subject) describe the unwelcome nature of change, albeit often necessary change, in their organisations. They describe concerns over further outplacement, more de-layering, more budget cuts, highly challenging objectives, and greater pressure of work. Add to this the changing nature of work and workplace relationships, and the raw materials are in place for increased personal problems as well as a greater need for counselling to resolve them.

So whether someone is seeking your assistance or whether you are spotting out-of-character behaviour such as less patience or increased use of stimulants (for example, caffeine, nicotine, or alcohol) you probably need counselling skills within your repertoire.

Problems

Before we look at the gameplan I am recommending, let us look at the problems associated with counselling:

- *People in need of counselling often erect barriers around themselves.* These barriers can vary from denying the existence of a problem to blaming it on someone or something else. They see themselves as the only ones in step.

- *Our usual reaction, when we see someone's problem, is to be evaluative or interpretive.* We make a judgement about what we have been told or other assumptions without checking the facts. Alternatively we offer general sympathy but no help. This usual reaction is a natural tendency due to the 'recognition' ability of our brains. The effect is for us to offer an inappropriate solution or, even if it is the most appropriate solution, the very fact it is being suggested from 'outside the barrier' lessens the chance it will be accepted. This needs to be emphasised. When someone is in a situation where they need counselling, other people's suggestions are rarely accepted. They will always find a reason why a solution proposed by someone else is not right for them.

We need, therefore, an approach that identifies the cause of the problem, examines the options, and produces a 'home-grown' solution. These are the points around which the following game-plan is based.

1 Opening

The exact opening depends on whether the other person has approached you seeking help or you have approached them with the intention of raising the issue.

If they have approached you their anxiety will probably be apparent from their body language: worried expression, downcast eyes, quiet voice. If the problem is a serious one expect them also to look tired, as if they are sagging around the shoulders, because worry uses up a lot of energy. You need to signal that it is OK to talk. You may need to put down your pen, close the file you are looking at, or turn off your computer screen. You need to signal your readiness to listen by leaning back and looking relaxed, perhaps sitting asymmetrically, and to give them your full attention.

If you have approached them, on the other hand, you need to broach the subject, and this needs to be as non-accusatory and unemotive as possible. It also needs to be concise. The first thing to do is signpost you want to talk about something a bit sensitive: for example, 'John, there's something that's bothering me.

It's a bit sensitive. May I speak to you, please?' This will get their attention more than it will put them on the defensive. Next, two of the techniques described in the section on assertiveness will help. By *pointing out a discrepancy* you can raise the subject without accusing them of anything. 'John, I've noticed that you're drinking and smoking more than you used to. May I talk to you about it, please?' *Self-disclosure* will also help you. 'John, I have the impression that you're drinking and smoking more than you used to. I'm concerned. May I talk to you about it, please?' You will also need to choose your moment and the location. The other person needs to be relatively free to talk, and to do so in private.

Again you need to use body language to signal that you are not accusing them: neutral posture and tone of voice. But you also need to signal that you are serious about talking to them, so you may need to augment your eye contact with the 'broken record'. So after John denies he is drinking and smoking more than he used to, you could say, 'Maybe you're not, but I have the impression you are, so I would still like to talk to you about it.' You are not trying to out-argue them on the issue; simply signal that you will not be easily put off.

2 Your role as counsellor

Whether they have approached you or you have approached them, once the conversation has begun you can start to fulfil the role of counsellor. That role is to encourage the other person to talk and think rationally.

If they have approached you they are likely to talk with relative freedom. By gently probing and reflecting you will learn more about their problem, and they will start to think it through too.

If you have approached them you may need to begin with some closed questions, even some forced-choice questions, to encourage them to talk. (If you are unsure of what is meant by this, go back to the example in the section on probing and listening; see pages 38–51.) Then you can *probe* and *reflect*. This should get them thinking about potential options but, because you want them to 'buy into' their own solution, you may need to use some of the *round-up/reason/result* sequence of questions to help determine which of the options available to them will deliver what they want. You can use *hypothetical questions* to help them see the full benefit to themselves of implementing the solution. For example if John is drinking and smoking too much because of money troubles you could ask, 'So what would be the effect if you budgeted accurately and deliberately lived within your means?' or 'How would you feel in 12 months' time if you took steps now so that, by this time next year, your finances were straight again?' John, and only John, can come up with the motivation to do that: hence the importance of your not suggesting a solution yourself but using effective probing to steer John towards a solution of his own making.

A counselling conversation will only work in the right atmosphere, and an essential element of your role is to create and maintain it. It will come partly from the environment you create (hence the need to put down your pen, close the file etc) and partly from your body language. Much of it however will come from your style and speed of questioning. I once heard it described as 'trout-tickling'. Apparently, expert poachers can put their arm into a river and 'tickle' trout and salmon, lulling them into a feeling of security, and then literally cast them onto the river bank. If the poacher attempts to lift the fish out of the water too soon it will escape. He has no choice but to work at the pace of the fish rather than his own. While I would not suggest that, as a counsellor, you would want to trick the other person into a false sense of security you do want to give them a feeling of real security. You need to be calm and unhurried. Like the poacher you have no choice but to work at their pace rather than your own. It is the epitome of 'pulling' rather than 'pushing'.

3 Commitment to a solution

If counselling is to be successful, two things are needed – a solution, and commitment to it. It would be easy to stop once the other person has come up with a viable solution. An essential part of the gameplan, however, is to keep going until commitment is established. So, returning to our example of John and his money troubles, let us say that, with your prompting, he came up with the solution of doing some accurate budgeting and then seeing his bank manager to seek help over consolidating credit-card loans into a cheaper overdraft and maintaining discipline over its repayment. Very gently, you need to keep probing. When will

John start the budget? What will he have to do to complete it? What help will he need and from whom will he need it? When will the budget be ready? When will he telephone the bank manager to make an appointment? How will he open the meeting? Will he let you know how he is getting on? When? How will he avoid slipping back into trouble?

You have to be careful when asking these questions. If you fire them off too quickly you will sound like an interrogator and the other person will start to get defensive. Tread softly but persistently. Be prepared to paraphrase questions that do not get answered. Be prepared to pause and wait for an answer. This will signal your intention to persist. You need to see commitment from the other person. Helping them break down the solution into small, manageable tasks is the best way of establishing that commitment.

Towards the end of the session try asking the hypothetical question, 'And how do you think you'll feel when all this trouble is behind you?' That is the goal for which the other person is aiming. That, and a reminder you are available whenever they need help, is a nice way of rounding off. Add to that a little praising for the way they have approached the conversation and you will be ending on a high note. (See Table 5.4 on page 162.)

Conclusion

Work on the basis that the solution and the motivation to do something about it are locked inside the other person. The key is on the inside and you have to encourage them to open it. To do that you need to create the right atmosphere by listening well and giving non-verbal signals. Then your reflective probing will encourage the other person to talk, and your open questions and hypothetical questions will draw them towards a conclusion.

Giving bad news to someone

Introduction

Of all the tasks faced by people at work, giving bad news to someone must be one of the most daunting. In our minds, it is conflict waiting to happen.

Table 5.4
Counselling to resolve a personal problem

1 Opening	• Signpost; self-disclosure ie mention it is 'something causing me concern'. • Be concise; point out a discrepancy. • Use eye contact and, if necessary, the 'broken record'.
2 Your role as counsellor	• Reflecting, gentle probing. • A lot of listening and encouraging. • Relaxed, receptive posture.
3 Commitment to a solution	• Hypothetical questioning. • Round up reasons; sell benefits. • Action planning; gentle persistence. • Praise.

The scope for bad news is however increasing. At the time of writing (1994) company after company seems to be shedding jobs even in traditionally 'safe' areas such as some head-office functions and seemingly secure strata of the hierarchy. Sometimes this is a reaction to falling business and at other times is a result of changes such as decentralisation, federalisation, empowerment, and re-engineering. Careers too are less predictable as tall, thin organisational structures become short and flat with consequent disappointment for those whose mind-set is geared to a former situation. Money, or the lack of it, seems to be more of an issue than it was a decade ago not only in absolute terms but also because, as the seemingly relentless march of performance-related pay continues, more managers are having to say 'no' to their staff; automatic annual increases cease to be the commonplace they once were. In short you need to be good at giving bad news. But that does not make it any the less daunting.

Problems

Consider the following problems:

• *Knowing far in advance we have to pass on bad news sends*

162

our minds into overdrive about how awful it is going to be. Such self-talk is usually prone to exaggeration, making out that the situation will be worse than it really is. The self-fulfilling prophecy ensures however that it is at least that bad!

- *This negative self-talk makes us sugar-coat the message so that we ourselves feel better.* One way of doing this is to beat about the bush, dragging out the actual announcement of the bad news and postponing the potential discomfort. This probably unnerves the other person more than a blunt message.

- *Sometimes we just do not stop talking.* We deliver the message, explain the reason for it, explain we know how the other person is feeling and describe what they need to do now, all without any involvement from the other person. It is almost as if we are afraid that the moment we stop talking they will start and that is when the confrontation will begin. So if we do not stop talking the problem will not arise. We put off what we fear most, rush the other person, and make an unhappy situation worse.

- *We seek comfort behind phrases that hide our real meaning.* One of the all-time greats has to be, 'We're going to have to let you go,' as if the poor employee to whom we are talking has been straining at the leash for years waiting for the first opportunity to get free. What we really mean is, 'You're fired and I know you feel pretty sick about it; I just don't have the guts to come right out and say it.' More 'up-beat' varieties include '. . . affected by the recent skill-mix adjustments' and '. . . at variance with our future competency requirements'. The result is confusion and resentment.

In any situation where bad news is being delivered the outcome will never be pleasant. Rather than make matters worse we should however aim to minimise the other person's discomfort and, in so doing, minimise our own. A good measure of how effectively you deliver bad news is when the other person thanks you for the way you handled the announcement.

Let us turn now to the gameplan.

1 Prepare

Depending on the severity of the bad news the other person may be in a state of shock when you tell them. So, before you begin, put in place a support plan. In the case of redundancy, for example, it will be little use sending them back to their desks and expecting them to carry on as if nothing had happened. After you have made the announcement will someone be available to give them help and advice? Who will look after their work for the rest of the day or week? Put these plans in place before the discussion is held.

2 Signpost

If you act at all unusually the other person will pick up from your body language that something is amiss. Their thoughts will start racing as to what it could be, so it is far better to focus those thoughts at the beginning. Say, for example, 'Sandra, I need to talk to you for a moment. It's something important. Would you come in, please?' Your tone of voice and facial expression will indicate that it is something unpleasant.

3 Give the reason, then the outcome

'As you know, the company has been looking at staffing levels in relation to business forecasts and decided that we needed a 10 per cent reduction in head-count. Unfortunately, not enough volunteers have come forward and so there will be some compulsory redundancies. Everyone within five years of retirement age is to retire early. You come into that category, Sandra, so I am sorry to have to tell you that, from the end of next month, your job will be redundant.' If you give the news first and then the reason behind it, the reason is lost. It is like signposting a disagreement: no one listens to the reasons why. You may also find that, because we think much faster than someone talks, when presenting the information this way, they will get to the outcome slightly ahead of you.

Notice, please, that giving the reason first, then the outcome, need not take a long time. The example above takes about 12 seconds to say. Compare that with the way some people ramble on for a minute or so, deferring the actual announcement.

4 Listen

Having heard the bad news the other person's first reaction may be one of shock. Their thoughts are racing. They do not know what to say so they do not say anything. Neither should you. Give them time. Eventually they will speak and you will need to listen, but probably more passively than actively. Depending on the news they may be angry, sad, or any of a number of other feelings. They may give vent to their feelings by verbally attacking you. Remember that their emotions are running high and they may not speak kindly. So stay in control of your own emotions and do not take what they are saying personally.

5 Maintain the focus

Again, depending on the type of bad news, they may try to debate the issue. Stay focused, using the 'broken record' if necessary, and encourage them to stay focused too. 'Yes, you have been here a long time but the decision has been taken and your job is to be made redundant'; 'Yes, I know it feels unfair but the decision has been taken. It affects everyone in your age group.'

Use gentle probing to encourage them to focus their thoughts on future needs rather than on what have, abruptly, become past ones. If there is any assistance you can give (such as in this case redundancy counselling or pre-retirement planning) describing it now will help with the future focus.

6 Put the support plan into action

Put into action the support plan and keep informed of how it is progressing.

Conclusion

Giving bad news to someone is an unpleasant task but often an unavoidable one. It is essential that it is handled sensitively and efficiently. You will know you have got it about right when the person to whom you have given the bad news thanks you for the way you handled the situation.

Table 5.5
Giving bad news to someone

1 Prepare	• Put together a support plan.
2 Signpost	• Signpost that it will be an out-of-the-ordinary discussion; serious body language. • Be brief.
3 Give the reason, then the outcome	• Be concise. • Neutral tone of voice and posture; keep eye contact. • Watch their body language.
4 Listen	• Listen more passively than actively. • Stay in control of your emotions no matter what the 'packaging'.
5 Maintain the focus	• Acknowledge what they are saying. • Use 'broken record' to stay focused. • Gentle probing.
6 Put the support plan into action	• Action the plan and monitor its progress.

Coaching to improve performance

Introduction

Ask yourself who, in a soccer match, scores the goals. Is it the players or the coach? You could ask the same question for any other sport. Once the game starts, the coach, the manager, and all the other 'support staff' sit on the sidelines and it is the players who get on with the game; so too with much of today's work activity. In the Introduction (Chapter 1) I made the point about success depending on people who, not so long ago, were thought of simply as order fodder. A company's customer-care policy, for example, depends more on a delivery-van driver than it does on the chief executive. Yet far too many people are stuck in a mind-set that is two or three decades out of date:

they forget who has to perform once the whistle blows.

Modern management is less about controlling and more about enabling. Modern leadership is less about being a charismatic and infallible superior and more about promoting change and improving performance by healthy collaboration at any and every level in an organisation. In this context coaching is a concept whose time has come. Whether you are a senior manager who has to translate vision into reality, a junior manager who wants to improve staff performance without spending money on training courses, or a specialist who is expected to 'bring on' less experienced people, you and your staff will benefit from effective coaching.

Coaching is the process of helping someone improve their performance. It is based on a few sound principles:

- Someone's job, if viewed the right way, is a significant source of learning opportunities.
- Shared learning is usually more effective, and easier to sustain than solo learning.
- You cannot teach anyone anything; all you can do is help them learn.

Furthermore, done properly it is virtually guaranteed to improve performance. It costs nothing other than a bit of time. In fact it rarely takes extra time; it just means changing the style of conversations that take place anyway. It improves relationships, trust and confidence, and encourages continuous learning. In fact if it is that good why don't more managers do it? The answer is that problems tend to get in the way.

Problems

Here are the main ones:

- *People do not see it as part of their job.* They are still operating on a mind-set that says staff are there to enable managers to get on with their jobs. That is like a soccer coach believing the real work goes on during practice sessions while the matches fans pay to see are not so important. The nature of most of today's jobs demands on the contrary that it is the staff who perform and

167

that the manager is there to enable the staff to perform well.

- *People misunderstand the nature of coaching.* This is hardly surprising because many professional coaches also misunderstand it. They assume that coaching is about teaching rather than helping someone learn. There is a big difference. In the one view the learner is seen as an empty vessel into which advice from the coach is poured. In the other the learner is like a seed, such as an acorn, capable of growth if nurtured the right way. This distinction is critical. In the first view the coach is seen as a *topic* expert. In the other, the coach is seen as a *process* expert.

Let me explain with some anecdotes. I was once running a course in a company where the main social activity was competitive hockey. The team had not been playing too well recently but the manager knew David Whitacker of Performance Consultants and asked him to take a coaching session. (David was the coach who took the English men's hockey team from nowhere to a gold medal at the Seoul Olympics.) I asked how it went.

– It was the strangest coaching session we've ever had, responded one of the guys in the team.

– In what way? I asked.

– He watched us play for about 20 minutes, then took us into the dressing room.

– And there he told you how to improve?

– No. He just asked us question after question after question.

– For how long?

– About one-and-a-half hours.

– What sort of questions?

– About why we did what we did, how we could do it differently, what we were thinking when we were playing, what effect those thoughts were having . . . and lots of others.

– And has it done any good?

– Haven't lost a game since!

Now David Whitacker is an expert hockey player – but he is also an expert coach. He knew that the answer to the team's playing problems had to be theirs. His role was therefore to help them sort it out.

One of David's colleagues from Performance Consultants, John Whitmore, has been known to coach good-standard golfers to improve performance – which does not sound odd until you learn that he is a racing-car driver, not a golfer. He just also happens to be an expert coach.

On one of my coaching courses I once asked the participants, after I had covered the basics of coaching, to pair up and coach one another in a topic about which the coach knew nothing but the learner did. (This way I knew the coach would have to rely on the coaching gameplan and not on any subject knowledge.) One of the course participants was a keen scuba-diver who instructed novice divers at weekends. His coach, who had never done any scuba-diving in his life, successfully coached him in improving his method of teaching underwater safety procedures.

Coaching is then about helping someone learn, not about teaching them, which means that the coach has to be first and foremost good at the process of coaching rather than good at the subject in hand.

- *Lack of patience.* It is much quicker to give a solution to someone than to help them work it out for themselves. The problem is however more one of perceived priorities than of absolute time. The benefit of helping someone work out a solution for themselves is not recognised.

Anyone who thinks otherwise would do well to heed the examples of two well-known figures. One is John de Lorean, the former motor-car manufacturer. He was at one time the youngest vice-president in General Motors' history; when he reached the dizzy heights of corporate HQ he found he could not get any work done because his staff kept bringing him problems they expected him to solve. His response was to send them all a memo saying that, from that time on, no one was to bring him a problem unless it was accompanied by at least two potential solutions. The number of problems halved overnight as people started working out solutions for themselves. The second example comes from Sir John Harvey-Jones, the former chairman of ICI. He reasons that if he had simply given his staff answers to their problems he would probably have given them yesterday's solutions, because it was some while since he had done their jobs. If on the other hand he helped them work out answers for themselves he would help them discover tomorrow's solutions.

There may well be occasions when it is sensible to hand someone an answer on a plate. On most occasions it will however be better to help them work it out for themselves. Not only might it be a better solution but they may well be able to apply that thinking to other problems in the future, benefiting both you and them.

- *Lack of skills.* Encouraging someone to think, to analyse, and to visualise requires the sorts of skills described in this book – probing, listening, awareness of body language, and so on – which not all managers have or use.

If you are going to coach someone successfully, you need to recognise that it is time well spent, that it uses the skills you have been reading about in this book, and that it takes a certain mind-set concerning your role. You are the helper, not the fount of all wisdom. You also need a framework within which to work. While there are several frameworks related to coaching I find the one advocated by John Whitmore in his book *Coaching for Performance* (London, Nicholas Brealey, 1992) and used by Performance Consultants (John Whitmore, David Whitacker and David Hemery, the former Olympic hurdler) both useful and easy to remember. It uses the Mnemonic 'GROW'. For the record, I have made a slight amendment in the final part. Here it is as part of the coaching gameplan:

1 Follow a framework

'GROW', the mnemonic advocated by Performance Consultants (with my amendment), stands for **G**oal, **R**eality, **O**ptions, and **W**ay forward.

Begin with the end in mind. Establish a *Goal.* Have something to aim for. It might be to cost a particular project for the first time, to take your place at an important meeting, to deliver better sales presentations, or to become professionally qualified. Without a goal to aim for, planning and motivation suffer. These are *end goals*: what this particular piece of coaching is intended to deliver eventually. Coaching also benefits from *process goals*, the 'milestones' that need to be achieved along the way. Costing a project may involve the learner in seeking information on suppliers, material costs, cash flow and borrowing, critical path analysis etc. Acquiring a professional qualification might involve writing to professional bodies, reading their literature, talking to a variety of professionals, deciding which qualification to go for etc. *Session goals* are also useful. Deciding what will be achieved by the end of a particular discussion between coach and learner provides focus for the meeting.

Like all goals, coaching goals need to be descriptive rather than qualitative. 'To deliver better sales presentations' is not as helpful as 'to deliver sales presentations in which I am relaxed, knowledgeable and which focus on the benefits to the audience of buying my product'. Being this specific helps visualisation of the goal, which is essential to lasting motivation.

Once you have a goal, you can explore the relevant *Reality*: What the situation looks like now. Goals establish where the learner wants to get to. It is important the learner understands where they are now. So looking at the sales presentation goal you might need to ask questions such as, 'How do you currently prepare for a sales presentation?' or 'How do customers react when you say that?' An important theme running throughout Performance Consultants' work is that *the mind is the key*, so be prepared to probe into the learner's thoughts and feelings: ask, 'What goes through your mind when a customer raises an objection during a sales presentation?' and 'What effect do those thoughts have on you?'

Probe deeply and listen well. Concentrate on behaviours and thoughts, not on attributes. The learner is seeking to turn their desires into reality. Only behaviour will perform the link. To know what to do they need to consider the *Options*.

There is normally more than one way to achieve a goal. Helping the learner identify and work through the options has several benefits. First, they become a thinker. They get into the habit of thinking things through, particularly with regard to the *consequences* of a course of action. You can help them with hypothetical questions: 'If you come across as too confident in a sales presentation, how do you think customers might react?' or 'If you mention a price at that stage, where will people's attention be when you talk about benefits?' Second, they develop confidence and commitment towards the option they do select.

It is important that you continually tease out the learner's thoughts with questions rather than suppress them with statements. I have heard the coaching process described as 'a voyage of discovery'. Certainly adults tend to learn more and retain that learning better when they have worked it out for themselves. Questioning assists this process. It is often referred to as 'the Socratic method' because it is how Socrates, the Greek philosopher, taught his students. It is also central to a lot of the accelerated-learning techniques trainers are employing these days.

The point about confidence and commitment is worth emphasising. If, when coaching, you are helping someone learn (as opposed to teaching them) you need to do three things: focus their *attention* on the issue under discussion; raise their *awareness* of the processes involved in that issue; and encourage them to take *responsibility* to achieve their goals. Just as in selling, it is the learner who has to make the decisions and the commitment. Questioning assists that process.

Finally you need to help the learner establish the *Way forward*. Just as in counselling, detailed questions about what will happen, when it will happen, what help is needed from whom, and so on will help establish commitment. It has the added benefit of breaking down large, complex tasks into more management steps.

2 Employ the skills

From what I have said under Point 1 above you will no doubt have already formed the opinion that *probing and listening* are key coaching skills. You will need to use the full range of productive questions and to listen a great deal. You will also need to exercise a great deal of self-control. It is not easy to sit there listening to someone trying to work something out for themselves when you feel you could save a great deal of time by simply giving them the answer. So please remember that the more thinking-skills you give them now, the more they can apply those skills to new and different situations in the future; that is compliment indeed to your skills as manager/leader.

You will also need to watch their *body language* so that you can detect signs of anxiety, or indeed confidence, and respond accordingly. Your own body language will need to support your listening and probing.

3 Make it part of your *modus operandi*

Coach regularly and coach naturally. Make it part of your normal activity – the way you do things. Staff appraisal fails in many or-ganisations because it is a once-a-year activity 'bolted onto' other management tasks. With coaching, you have an opportu-nity to improve the way you manage. While I would be delighted to see more managers set aside times for special meetings la-belled 'coaching' I feel there is more to be gained from changing the style of discussions that already take place.

Most managers meet their staff to review progress of particu-lar tasks, listen to situation reports, and look at the monthly fig-ures; they travel with them to attend meetings and walk down corridors with them. These are all naturally occurring coaching opportunities. Even when a member of staff comes in to ask you something, try these three questions:

- What is a clear statement of the problem?
- What are the alternatives?
- What would you recommend and why?

You will also find them beneficial if you and your staff answer them before discussing problems with other people.

Delegation

One final point remains to be covered under this section on management *modus operandi*. It concerns delegation. While coaching is by no means confined to delegated tasks delegation works better when managers understand coaching. It is only natural to be anxious when delegating something to a member of staff for the first time. Unfortunately some managers use that anxiety to convince themselves that delegating compli-cated tasks is too risky. Consequently their staff do not develop and they end up doing more than they need to. If you come into that category you may like to consider 'The Manager's

173

Table 5.6
Coaching to improve performance

---

1 Follow a framework:

– Goal	• Remember the Socratic method – use questioning to make the learner think. • Use end-, process- and session goals.
– Reality	• Listen actively; probe. • Raise the learner's awareness.
– Options	• Use hypothetical questions. • Control urge just to tell them. • Draw out the consequences of what they are saying. • Use body language to show that you are unhurried.
– Way forward	• As with counselling, help create an action plan and gain their commitment to it. • Ask hypothetical questions. • Praise.
2 Do it regularly	• Make it part of your management style. • Remember 'Manager's Insurance Policy'.

Insurance Policy'. It involves categorising tasks according to the following list:

Category 1 It's mine. Don't touch! I'm the only one who can do this.

Category 2 It's mine. You can try some of it so we'll discuss the problems, the options, and the likely courses of action.

Category 3 It's yours but, as you're still learning, check with me before you put decisions into practice.

Category 4 It's yours but I want regular and frequent reporting.

Category 5 It's yours. I trust you with it so all I need is
exception-reporting.

This approach has two effects. First, it means that delegation
need not be all or nothing. Second, by planning to elevate a task
from one category to another, it gives you and the learner goals
to aim for.

Conclusion

Coaching is based on sound principles: work is full of learning
opportunities; learning that is shared is better, and easier to sustain; and people learn rather than get taught. Effective coaches
are coaching experts rather than subject experts. By using effective questioning they focus the learner's attention, raise their
awareness of how they perform and harness their commitment to
better performance.

Handling people who cause you delays

Introduction

One of the features of organisational life is that there are times
when we depend on other people and they let us down. Here is
a short gameplan suggesting how you might handle such
people:

Problems

There are several:

- *Our frequent reminders have no effect.* The people who have
  let us down seem immune to them.
- *We approach them in a sympathetic way hoping for the co-
  operation we need.* The result is that we feel bad for being so
  wimpish and they still fail to give us what we want.
- *We send a last-ditch memo with veiled threats of what will*

happen if their co-operation 'is not forthcoming'. It does not come forth and we don't carry out our threats because we know it means losing face.

- *Eventually, although we need their co-operation, they have so annoyed us we go in with both guns blazing.* The result is that we feel good temporarily but still fail to get what we want.

Here is a suggested gameplan. It may not work every time but it will work enough of the time to be of value.

1 Write it down

See the person who is letting you down face to face and, when you have agreed what assistance they are going to provide, write it down and let them see you writing it down. Written commitments are always stronger than verbal ones.

2 Appeal to their sense of honour

Ask them straight: 'Can I count on you for that?' Look them directly in the eye and nod as you ask the question. As we tend to mirror another person's body language, they will probably nod as they confirm that you can indeed count on them.

3 Use subtle 'bribery'

There is a saying in negotiating that goes, 'trade, don't concede'. That is why you will hear negotiators say things like 'If you [do this], I'll [do that]' and 'I can only agree [to this] if you can agree [to that].' You can use this principle to 'bribe' the other person: 'If you bring me that information on the 17th, I'll buy you a [beer, coffee, or whatever it is worth].' (Notice the confirmation of the date by which you agreed the information would be supplied.)

You can add to this bribery by a subtle little change: instead of '*If* you bring me . . .' you can say, '*When* you bring me . . .'. This creates a more positive and permanent vision in the other person's mind.

4 Explain the benefits

Most of us do things because we perceive a personal benefit in it. It might be that we feel good when we help someone, or that we know we would feel guilty if we did not. You will know the person from whom you want this information and also whether they need more tangible benefits. If the information they are providing is substantial maybe they deserve a bigger reward than a cup of coffee or a glass of beer. So, if appropriate, you can finish off the 'bribery' sentence with '. . . and I'll tell your boss how helpful you've been'. This also carries the implication that if they do not deliver the information by the agreed date you will pass on that news instead.

5 Thank them

If the event has been significant enough a short praising might be appropriate here. (You feel good when you know you can rely on them, you know this report will be a good team-effort, you know the customer will appreciate the amount of work that has gone into it etc.) At the very least they deserve a genuine thank-you. That means one given with a smile, eye contact, and an attentive posture (not delivered over your shoulder on the way out of their office).

Table 5.7
Handling people who cause you delays

1 **Write it down**	• This adds to their commitment.
2 **Appeal to their sense of honour**	• Make eye contact; nod so that they 'mirror'.
3 **Use subtle 'bribery'**	• 'When you . . . , I'll . . .'
4 **Explain the benefits**	• Be very concise.
5 **Thank them**	• Make eye contact; smile. • Self-disclosure. • Pause.

Conclusion

This approach may look contrived. It is however preferable to being aggressive, submissive, moaning, or complaining to their boss etc. Try to use it naturally and it will have positive effects.

Negotiating

Introduction

People who attend my courses tell me they are doing more negotiating than in the past or that they have had to start negotiating for the first time. There are several reasons for this increase. Responsibility for purchasing may have been delegated to line managers, so they are negotiating with suppliers. Budgets are becoming tighter so externally managers are pushing for bigger discounts while internally fighting for resources. Finally, flatter organisations tend to lend themselves to more of a matrix style of management, with constantly shifting teams, so people find themselves negotiating with colleagues over resources, staff, time-scales, availability, and so on.

Problems

Negotiating is a new skill for many people, and one that is easy to approach the wrong way. Here are the problems I come across most frequently:

- *Mind-set.* This is the big one from which all the other problems stem. People see the process as a kind of tug-of-war where what one party gains the other, by definition, has to lose. This encourages them to try several different tactics:
  - They may try to attempt to manipulate or trick the other party. When dealing with a salesperson, for example, they may keep him or her waiting, suddenly but deliberately cut short the meeting on a pretext, leave a competitor's brochure just visible in a strategic position and demand

'your best price!' When dealing with someone internally they may try to pull rank, to flatter, or to present a logical argument to convince the other person that their cause is more essential to organisational success than the other person's. (Sales and finance are two functions that are often pretty quick with this one.)

- They may try to gain concessions with tricks, threats, and posturing. Pretending to withdraw from the negotiations if their 'very reasonable' demands are not met is a favourite. Telling lies is another. A colleague once told me about some wage negotiations he attended. He was seated next to the personnel director, the lead negotiator. Apparently the negotiations became heated and the union representatives threatened to walk out unless their demands were met, whereupon the personnel director took out his calculator and begged them not to leave, while he feverishly recalculated all his figures. He even managed to sweat as he went through pages of calculations muttering something about really sticking his neck out and his job being on the line. His index finger danced across the calculator as he said that he could not fully match the union's demands but could get close to them, assuming he still had a job when the chief executive discovered what he was about to agree to. The union representatives accepted his offer and the negotiations closed. My colleague noticed that throughout all the theatricals the personnel director's calculator wasn't even switched on!

That was the spirit of the 1970s. Things were different in the late 1980s, when I had the pleasure of working with an international oil company. The employee relations director told me that wage negotiations used to be characterised by several days and nights of huffing and puffing, beer and sandwiches, and midnight oil. On a recent occasion, however, management had met the union representatives and said, 'We'll show you what a "win" looks like to us, and explain why, if you will show us what a "win" looks like to you, and explain why.' The negotiations ended amicably the same day.

- *People making goodwill concessions on the assumption they will be reciprocated.* Usually the reverse happens: it convinces the other person that if they sit tight, more concessions will follow.

What we need is therefore a gameplan that facilitates co-operation without leaving us exposed or committed to unilateral concessions.

1 Question in order to broaden

There are four potential outcomes to any negotiation: win/lose, lose/win, lose/lose and win/win. Unless you are dealing with the release of hostages or some such other extreme situation there is only one outcome worth considering – win/win. Fundamental to negotiating is the principle of trading rather than conceding. By trading creatively you can handle negotiations to achieve a win/win even when the other party is thinking solely of win/lose. Before you can begin to trade, however, you need to broaden the issue under discussion, and to do that you need to question, question, question.

Using the round-up/reason/result approach we covered under persuasive selling (see pages 61–75) you can find out what is important to the other person. This will enable you to do two things. First, you can identify the other person's perception of value. If you have something they value then you have good bargaining power, especially if that something will cost you little. For example if a speedy delivery is critical to the other person and your delivery van will be in their area tomorrow, your bargaining power has just gone up. If they want your subject-matter expert next week, and the project on which she is currently working is due to end this Friday, your bargaining power has just gone up. If the safety implications of a new directive are important to the other person, and you have the only safety expert in the company, your bargaining power has just gone up. But you will only discover these things if you question on a broad front. To broaden the discussion you may need to signpost well. Try questions such as 'I'd like to make sure I understand the background to this discussion. May I ask you a few general questions, please?' This may do the trick.

2 Link in order to trade

Often, to give yourself more bargaining power you need to be creative about what you link together when you start trading. By way of illustration, the usual items that salespeople link are price and volume: 'I can increase the discount only if you increase the quantity you order.' They could also add in other aspects of the deal such as time-scales to delivery, storage of the goods, warranties, after-sales service, returns policies, money-back guarantees, and even add in aspects of the relationship such as technical advice, staff training, marketing endorsements, referrals, first opportunity to tender for the next deal etc, etc. All it takes is a little lateral thinking, which is easily stimulated by the amount of questioning you do.

3 Stick to the core skills

Negotiating is one of those activities where all five core skills are needed throughout (see pages 36–38). You need to probe and listen. All the productive questions have a role in the negotiating and you need to listen actively. Open questions, reflecting, and pausing will encourage the other person to talk. Hypothetical questions will help test the water and are especially useful when you start trading. Closed questions are useful for checking. Summarising and checking your understanding, especially when used with signposting and self-disclosure, will not only help you stay on the same wavelength: they will help you be seen as open and honest.

Remember the behaviour triggers and responses described in the section on fundamental principles (see Table 2.1). Avoid proposing, disagreeing, and stating difficulties wherever possible and use the more productive triggers such as seeking ideas, making suggestions, building, and supporting.

Control of your own body language and awareness of the other person's are vital. You want to give away little with your own 'non-verbals' as well as ensure that the other person supports the words you are speaking. I once observed a negotiating role play between a young female scientist and an estate agent. He was winning easily, yet she was doing everything according to the book – except for one thing. I stopped the role play after about 10 minutes and privately pointed out to her that every time she wanted to make a serious point she averted her gaze to the table. I asked her to make deliberate eye contact with every serious sentence. The role play resumed and the estate agent capitulated after two minutes. His comment, when I asked him why he gave up so soon, was interesting. He said, 'This time she means it.' Even more interesting was that he could not tell me how he knew – he just knew! Your eye contact, tone of voice, posture, and gestures all need to be positive.

As you observe the other person's body language watch for clusters of disapproval (leaning back, arms folded, head tilted back slightly), lying (eye shiftiness, hand to back of neck), impatience (tight lips, loud exhalation, faster breathing), consideration (chin-stroking, upward gaze), and so on.

Remember the key lessons of assertiveness. As well as controlling tone of voice and eye contact be concise rather than rambling, be prepared to say what you want, and use the 'broken record' to stand your ground while encouraging movement from the other person.

Table 5.8
Negotiating

1 **Question in order to broaden**	• Probe and listen. • Round up as much information as possible. • Look for benefits to the other person that cost *you* little. • Weigh up your bargaining power.
2 **Link in order to trade**	• Be creative; think relationship as well as product or service.
3 **Stick to the core skills**	• Ask for ideas about what they want. • Build on those ideas. • Suggest rather than propose. • Use hypothetical questions to test trade-offs: 'If I . . . , will you . . . ?' • Maintain a relaxed posture; eye contact is especially important for serious remarks. • Use the 'broken record' to encourage movement on the other person's part.

Avoid the no-noes of talking too much, using 'red rag' words and phrases, making counter-proposals, facilitating defend/attack spirals, stacking up too many arguments in your favour, and persistent use of the 'royal we' and formalspeak.

Conclusion

Negotiating is not a tug-of-war. When it does become one, relationships and effectiveness deteriorate. It is instead about trading and creativity. When these two characteristics are evident it is often possible to arrive at a better joint solution than either party could have dreamed up independently.

Resolving a difference of opinion

Introduction

This section has many similarities to that on negotiating, so rather than repeat too much here I will assume you have already read the preceding section. As with negotiating, the scope for differences of opinion is increasing. All the reasons applying to negotiating apply here but there is one more worth emphasising.

Uncertainty follows in the wake of change and there cannot be many organisations that have not experienced significant change in recent years. Many old ways of working and of doing things have either been swept aside and replaced with new ones or are at least on the retreat. In some cases they have just been swept away and replaced with nothing in particular. In such an environment people are more prone to differences of opinion, because their opinions have not been standardised by long-standing custom and practice.

Differences of opinion can exist with staff, colleagues, bosses, suppliers, customers, officials and almost anyone else. Where the difference is slight or of no consequence you might safely live with it. Where it is significant, however, it will need to be addressed and with luck resolved before progress can be made.

I believe there is no problem with differences of opinion. In fact it is often healthy. If people do not disagree, how are current methods and attitudes ever to be challenged? The problem is more in the *way* conflict and differences of opinion are managed and resolved.

Problems

Again there are problems. Many are the same as those for negotiating, but here are two additional ones relevant to differences of opinion:

- *Some people have a win/lose mind-set.* They are incredibly competitive and adopt an adversarial approach even though they and the other person may be 'on the same side'. Aiming to win at the expense of the other person makes little sense. Whether they are a colleague, a customer, or a supplier they are all part of the same extended team. Where significant principles are at stake a steadfast approach may be admirable, but where organisational effectiveness is at stake it is egocentric.
- *Some people have a consensus mind-set and try not to rock the boat.* They see conflict as something to be avoided rather than as an energy which, if harnessed, can produce positive results. While the consensus approach may be relevant to some issues it can produce the proverbial camel when what we want is a racehorse. Reducing issues to the lowest common denominator is the road to mediocrity.

What we need is a mind-set that enables us to see what sort of differences we are dealing with, so that we can react accordingly.

Table 5.9
Differences of opinion and reactions to them

Type of difference:	small differences ●●●●●●●●●●●●●●●●●▶ of no consequence			huge differences of principle
Your reaction:	probably none	resolve by discussion	resolve by negotiation	remain steadfast

For small differences, all you might need to do is listen so as better to understand people. For bigger differences you may need to engage in discussion, listening to their viewpoint and explaining your own. As you move up the scale you may need to start trading and, finally, there may be some issues where you have to remain intransigent, explaining your viewpoint carefully. Each of these stages could be a separate discussion or represent different elements in the same discussion.

I feel this is a healthier way of looking at differences of opinion than thinking of them as win/lose or consensus. There is an additional viewpoint on resolving differences of opinion that also helps create a positive mind-set and points to productive behaviours with which to resolve those differences.

In almost any situation where there is a difference of opinion there is bound to be some area of *common interest*. Even if the only thing on which two people can agree is that a solution will require the agreement of them both, it is a start.

Here is an example. Let us say that the finance director of a company wants to cut costs and tighten up procedures. One area attracting his concern is the expenses enjoyed by the sales representatives. The sales director believes that a motivated team is a productive team and so he has always had a liberal view on expenses and even tolerates a little 'fudging' of expense claims. He even has a procedure in place whereby claims do not have to be substantiated until they reach a certain limit. He wants his people out selling, not worrying about receipts for car parking. After all, the company is in a precarious position and needs more sales. So what if they do exaggerate their claims a little? They work hard enough and, anyway, it is traditional for sales reps to fiddle a bit here and there! The finance director, on the other hand, believes in integrity in all money matters and would rather see higher commissions than tolerate expenses fiddling. He was brought in to help the company get out of a poor financial situation and intends to tighten up all financial procedures dramatically.

There two views appear to be diametrically opposed but if we look at them in detail – in Table 5.10 – we can see that there is a degree of overlap.

If the finance and sales directors in the example were at all typical they would see their differences as a trial of strength and probably seek a political solution by trying to get the chief executive on their individual sides. The result would be a win/lose situation, a damaged relationship, and less organisational efficiency than there might otherwise be. An alternative would be

Table 5.10
Resolving differences – example of overlap

Finance director	Both	Sales director
• Believes in integrity and accuracy in all money matters.	• Better sales performance. • Healthy company performance. • Confidence in each other.	• Believes in traditional approach to expenses.
• Wants tight procedures, accurate expense claims, financial integrity, confidence in sales reps' expenses.		• Believes tolerance of expense 'fudging' essential to motivation.
		• Wants happy sales force, no imposed controls, no interference.

for one of them at least to begin with some broad questioning, *rounding up* as much information as possible to find out why the other wants what they want, on what beliefs they are basing their approach, and what *benefits* they see in that. Then to *build* on the other's responses and make *suggestions* using *hypothetical questions* so that the other sees the cause and effect between what they want and the solution being proposed. In this example the sales director might be able to persuade the finance director that the amount of money that would be saved by tightening up on sales reps' expenses would result in less time in front of customers which would have in turn a detrimental effect on sales performance.

The trick to resolving a difference of opinion is first seeking to understand and then seeking to be understood. So the gameplan would look like this:

1 Probe and listen

Listen to the other person's proposal, probe to find out what they want from it, how they see their proposal delivering what they want, and on what beliefs they are working. Use open questions to gain information and closed questions to check your understanding. Control your body language so you come across as someone who is seeking to understand rather than interrogate, or as someone who is signalling disagreement. Signposting will help.

The very least that will happen is that if you do need to dig in and fundamentally disagree you will appear more reasonable than you would otherwise have done, because you will have listened and considered.

Table 5.11

Resolving a difference of opinion

1 Probe and listen	• Round up information. • Probe to understand both details and beliefs. • Search for benefits the other person hopes their proposal will bring. • Check your understanding.
2 Look for overlap	• Build on what the other person says they want. • Express your suggestions in terms of benefits to them. • Be prepared to trade. • Maintain a relaxed posture; eye contact is especially important for serious remarks. • Use the 'broken record' to encourage movement on their part.
3 Praise them	• Thank them for working with you to produce a solution from which company, customers or whoever will benefit.

2 Look for overlap

Look for areas where your interests coincide. Use building and suggesting to establish in the other person's mind the cause and effect between what they want and what you want (which might now be different from your reaction when you first heard what they wanted). Remember to express your suggestion in terms they will find attractive, that is, in terms of the benefits to them rather than in terms of the benefits to you or in terms of the features of your suggestion.

3 Praise them

When you reach an agreement, praise the other person in some way. They have listened and discussed and reconsidered their proposal. You want to encourage this behaviour so praise them for listening, for putting the company first, acting in the customers' interests, or whatever. That way, next time they may bounce their ideas off you first, thus giving you a better chance of altering their views while they are still fresh and before they begin to set hard.

Conclusion

As with negotiating, an adversarial approach is rarely productive. Neither is a consensus approach if it reduces ideas to their lowest common denominator. If we seek first to understand we will learn about the other person's motives and priorities and be likely to identify some common ground on which to build – producing with luck a worthwhile solution for everyone.

Persuading someone to use your services

Introduction

One of my clients, a substantial company with about 10,000 employees, used to have a training department that controlled the training budget and ran all the courses. It is now about one-half of its former size, line managers control their own training budgets, and the training department operates as a 'profit centre', promoting and selling its services throughout the company.

Similar trends are affecting personnel departments, marketing departments, data-processing departments, security departments, and many, many others. Sometimes an entire department finds itself competing against an outside supplier, sometimes external tenders are used to gauge the value for money an internal service provides, and sometimes commercial attitudes simply dictate that departments and the people within them let their internal customers know about the value they receive. More people wear a sales hat than realise it.

This section summarises and adds to the core skill of persuasive selling. It will be relevant to anyone who now has to sell their services either literally or metaphorically. It will also be useful to those of you who have to convince others of your recommendations. You are wearing a sales hat too because you want someone else to 'buy' your advice.

Problems

Here are the main problems. They were described in the section in Chapter 3 on persuasive selling, so I shall just summarise them here:

- *The assumption that, just because we can see the logic of our case, the other person will too.* This is the main fault here, from which all the others stem.
- *We forget that people buy something to fulfil a need.* Whether they are spending their own money or their department's budget, if they fail to see the need or fail to see that what you have to offer will satisfy their need, they will not be persuaded.
- *We present our case from **our** viewpoint and in **our** terms.* We describe what makes sense to us and what is attractive to us on the misguided assumption that it will also make sense to the other person and that they will find the same things attractive. We describe the features of the product or service and not the benefits those features will deliver to the other person. We use our jargon rather than theirs. As a result we widen the communication gap rather than close it.
- *We talk too much and listen too little.* We believe that giving information is an effective way of influencing – whereas, by asking the right questions and listening to the answers, we can find out exactly how to present our case.
- *We fail to spot the little signals that the other person is interested.* Questions such as 'Is it available in red?', 'How soon could you deliver?', 'If I agreed, how long would implementation take?' are the signs of interest.
- *We are 'thrown' by objections.* As soon as the other person disagrees with something that we say, or presents an obstacle to agreeing with us, we have difficulty handling it.

Effective influencers recognise these problems and overcome them by seeking to understand the other person's situation and problems, by involving the other person in the conversation and helping them appreciate fully how the product or service will benefit them. They do so by asking questions in a set sequence: see Figure 5.1.

Figure 5.1
Persuasive selling sequence

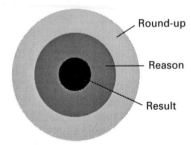

1 Round-up

Effective influencers first 'round up' information about the other person's situation, priorities and constraints. This is an information-gathering phase and may well need signposting as such to ensure that you and the other person are on the same wavelength. You could ask, 'Before I explain my proposal to you, may I put you a few questions to ensure that I understand your situation?'

If the other person is pressed for time or is in a rush to 'get down to business' you might have to persevere with the 'broken record'.

– Don't bother with the questions, just tell me what you've got to say.
– I'm happy to explain it to you, I just want to do so in terms that are relevant, so I'd still like to ask you a few questions, please.
– I'll be the judge of whether it's relevant.
– I know you will. However, there is usually more than one way of explaining something and I think it's in your interest that I explain it the right way for you and your situation, so I'd like to ask you a few questions, please.

The questions you ask will depend on what you are 'selling' and how much you already know. If the situation is brand-new to you, you may need to start very broadly with structure, business processes, objectives, plans, and constraints. If you are already familiar with the situation, you may just need to concentrate on the issue you are there to discuss. Either way you will want plenty of open questions, reflecting, checking that you understand, and summarising.

It is worth pointing out that customers often find that the process of you seeking information not only helps to clarify the situation in their minds but also helps them see proof that you are genuine in your recommendations.

2 Reason

Your round-up of information should with luck highlight areas that will prove fruitful for further probing. In the section in Chapter 3 on persuasive selling I presented the example of a computer salesman who discovered that his potential customer's current computer was slow, unreliable, and required too much manual intervention. The salesman then probed even further to determine the full implications of the problem which, in this case, were difficult month-ends, expensive contract staff, and dissatisfied customers: potential reasons for buying a new computer which the salesman mentally noted.

It is during this stage that summarising is particularly fruitful because you can use it to focus the other person's attention on the problem and its implications.

3 Result

'Result' refers to the benefits the customer will gain by buying your product or service. Or the benefit the other person will gain by agreeing to your proposal. There are two points to keep in mind during this stage. The first is to remember that a single compelling reason for doing something is a more powerful persuader than a whole stack of reasons. A whole stack of reasons can make you sound desperate and, because they are unlikely to be all as strong as one another, the other person can easily attack the weakest. So stick to a single compelling reason. You can always hold the others in reserve, should you need them.

The second point is that you want the other person to visualise the benefits they will gain. Visualisation can be a very powerful persuader – that is why so many advertisements on television and in magazines display a lifestyle, not just a product. The implication is that by chewing this gum you will become more carefree, by smoking these cigarettes you will gain greater enjoyment of the great outdoors, or by driving this motor car you will experience the charisma of a successful executive.

Hypothetical questions will help the other person visualise. Returning to our computer salesman, he asks the customer, 'What would be the effect on your need for contract staff if you had a reliable computer?' He knows that the use of contract staff is a concern of the customer's and that cost is another major concern. He knows these things because the customer told him in response to his questions. That is what the customer will '*buy*', even though he will *pay* for a computer.

Knowing what will be attractive to the customer is easier if you watch for *buying signals*. These are expressions of interest. They might be in the form of fairly obvious questions like those shown above eg 'How long would implementation take?' That kind of question shows interest because few people would enquire about implementation time-scales if they had already decided against implementation. Some buying signals, however, are more subtle. If in response to one of your points the other person exhibits a cluster of behaviours indicating consideration (finger and thumb to chin, head slightly inclined to one side, possibly with eyes looking upwards) it would be worth checking to see if you have just scored a point.

It is during this last stage that the other person may raise objections. Salespeople are often taught to *overcome* objections. This indicates a mind-set that sees objections as obstacles between you and 'sale'. Consequently salespeople are taught techniques to overcome the obstacles. A price objection, for example, might be tackled with a 'reduce to the ridiculous' tactic. A computer costing several thousand pounds might be 'too expensive' but one that 'costs only £2 a day', based on a four-year life, may not be.

A more productive mind-set is to think of objections as stepping-stones. If you satisfy the other person on a particular point you get that much closer to the decision. This attitude will encourage you to be more assertive. So if the other person says, 'I'd like to think about it' you might probe, 'What do you want to think about?' That way genuine objections are brought into the open and you can discuss them rationally. For example:

– I'm not sure. I'd like to think about it.
– That's fine. I'm glad you want to think about it. What exactly do you want to think about? We've established that your reduced use of contract staff will effectively pay for the computer so there will be no negative cash flow.
– There's a lot of change in the company at the moment. I'm wondering if my staff can handle learning a new computer.
– Is that the only thing you want to think about?
– Yes.
– If I can satisfy your concern on this issue is there anything else on which you would need reassurance?
– No, that would be it.
– OK, may I explain how the two computers compare?
– Please do.

Overcoming an objection with trickery is *not* the way to make a customer satisfied with the process or with the decision. Engaging them in rational discussion is much more productive and it is more acceptable to people who want long-term relationships.

Conclusion

We want the other person to be happy with both the decision and the process by which the decision was reached. Involving the other person while finding out what is important to them enables you to tailor your sales presentation to them. It also sets you apart from other persuaders because you will come across as genuine, a good listener, and someone who is working in the customer's interests as well as your own.

Table 5.12

Persuading someone to use your services

1 Round-up	• An information-gathering phase. • Signpost so the other person appreciates why you need to ask them so many questions. • Use open questions and reflecting.
2 Reason	• Continue probing to uncover the full extent of their problems and the issues they want to address. • Listen intently: they may not even realise the significance of some of the things they say.
3 Result	• Use hypothetical questions to help them see the full benefits that you are offering. • Look for 'buying signals'. • Probe objections.

Leading a productive meeting

Introduction

According to one piece of research I have come across, the average executive spends $16^1/2$ hours each week in meetings and rates one-third of them (ie more than six weeks a year!) unnecessary, unproductive, or in some other way a waste of time. Whether you are that average executive or whether you just know that the meetings you attend could be better managed there are time savings to be made from doing just that – managing them better.

There are other advantages too. Meetings are a bit of a 'shop window', especially when they are attended by someone senior. Some people like to show off in them to get noticed. The best way to get noticed is however to manage the process of the meeting, or to contribute towards the management of the meeting, positively.

While there is a general trend these days to do away with standing committees and consequently with their associated meetings I think it is fair to say that ever since the advent of quality circles there has been an increase in both the number of meetings and the types of people attending them. No longer are they simply the preserve of executives: they are also the domain of clerks and shop-floor workers. So if you chair meetings the whole of this section will be relevant. If you attend meetings you will still be able to identify tips relevant to your situation.

Problems

There can be many problems with meetings. Here are some of them:

- There is insufficient notice and hence insufficient preparation time.
- The start is postponed to allow latecomers to arrive; the time of punctual people is thus wasted. This is a good way of ensuring that meetings start later and later as more and more people choose not to waste time waiting. So they arrive when they think the meeting *will* start.
- Discussions ramble and people lose sight of why an item is on the agenda.
- The minutes take too long to prepare and are at variance with people's memories.
- They are staggeringly expensive. If you were to add up the employment costs of everyone at your next meeting you would probably be in for a shock.

Here is a gameplan that will help eradicate these problems:

1 Before the meeting

Distribute a *meeting plan* in sufficient time before the meeting. For a typical staff meeting three to five days ahead will probably be adequate. For, say, a strategy meeting three to five weeks would be necessary. The plan is a device to streamline the meeting. It should first state the purpose of the meeting. If it is not clear, cancel the meeting. Next, it should state *who* is attending and what *contribution* is expected from them. If they have no contribution, do they need to be there? If their attendance is due to their need to be informed why not let them have the minutes to read or an audiotape of the meeting which they can listen to in their car? Estimate the cost of the meeting by calculating approximate salaries plus on-costs (your personnel manager should be able to advise). Plus the expenses for the meeting. This tends to reduce the number of 'meeting groupies' who have no contribution but who feel obliged to say something once they are there. Finally, display an *objective agenda*. That is, for each item state why it is there – for example, 'To confirm marketing department's recommendation regarding . . .' or 'To choose one of the short-listed training providers' or 'To consider the issues involved in performance-related pay so that a circular can be produced for staff'. This helps you to stay on track.

2 During the meeting

First, unless there are specific and one-off reasons for not doing so, start on time. Do not wait for latecomers. Neither recapitulate for them. Take the important decisions first. This usually encourages punctuality.

Second, stay on track. Many of the skills we have covered will assist you – for example, *signposting*: 'Let's first of all look at all the good points in this proposal and then we'll look at the bad points'. Then *probing* when someone is straying: 'How does what you are saying relate to this item?' or 'How does what you are saying help us make this decision?' You are giving people a chance to justify themselves, which is fair. If they cannot your question will have more affect than a blunt 'Shut up'. *Summarising* is a very productive way of pulling together various aspects of the discussion either to check your understanding or to make a decision. Remember too that behaviours can trigger fairly predictable responses, so suggest rather than propose, and seek clarification rather than disagree. If you have to disagree directly do not signpost it; explain your reason first, then disagree.

If you have a choice, arrange the seating so that you can see everyone's body language. That way you can tell who wants to say something but is afraid to speak, who is confused but reluctant to ask, and who disagrees but does not say so.

Third, listen *actively* not only so that you can understand but also so that you can help less gifted contributors make their point. Also, avoid leading questions such as 'Right, does anybody want to disagree with me on this one?' If you are the most senior person there, that approach can be tempting.

Fourth, remember your role as conductor of the orchestra. If people mix suggesting, building, factual probing, negative thinking, and describing their feelings, the meeting will get out of tune, as it were. As the conductor, you can ensure harmony and progress by ensuring that everyone talks about only one aspect at a time. It might be worth rotating the chairperson role every meeting or appointing someone to act as *process manager*. Their role is to observe and comment on the process of the meeting but not to take part in it. Their input is to say things such as 'Jean made a relevant point there but it got lost in the general hubbub. It might be worth repeating' or 'You appear to be going around in circles on this one. Would you like me to summarise the opposing views so that you can make a decision?'

Finally, control time. Use the estimated cost figures to keep people on track – for example, remark that 'So far we've clocked up £200 discussing the relative merits of these two options. As the difference in cost between them is only £250 shall we make a decision?'

3 At the end of the meeting

Unless you need a verbatim record of the meeting for, say, legal reasons, keep the minutes to a minimum. Consider bullet-point minutes listing the decisions reached and who is responsible for what. Have them written as the meeting progresses, copied immediately the meeting ends, and distributed before people leave. Not only is it more efficient but it adds to the overall image of an efficiently run, no-nonsense meeting.

Conclusion

The number of meetings is increasing. Because they can be both expensive and ineffective they need to be handled carefully. In particular the *process* of the meeting needs managing and there are skills which, together with the right framework, enable us to do that.

Table 5.13

Leading a productive meeting

1 Before the meeting	• Distribute a meeting plan that states the meeting purpose; those who are to attend and their expected contribution; the cost and objectives of each agenda item.
2 During the meeting	• Start on time. • Take the important decisions first. • Use full range of core skills depending on agenda items (eg persuading, negotiating). • For process management, use signposting, probing, summarising, suggesting, and seeking clarification. • Observe others' body language. • Consider appointing a process manager.
3 At the end of the meeting	• Brief bullet-point minutes of decisions taken and who is responsible for what. • Distribute minutes at end of meeting.

Selecting the right candidate

Introduction

I once saw a thought-provoking advertisement for a recruitment agency. It said, 'If you think recruiting the right person is expensive, have you ever counted the cost of recruiting the wrong one?' People are not just an organisation's most valuable resource: they are often its most expensive, especially in the ever-growing service sector where there are no huge amounts of raw materials or production machinery. If someone is digging coal out of the ground we can measure how much they dig out each day. If someone is operating a widget machine we can count how many widgets pass the quality inspector. But if someone is working with their brain or working with relationships their output is more difficult to quantify. Hence the need to ensure that they have been properly selected and, as more recruitment and selection decisions are passed from personnel to line managers, more people will need selection skills.

Problems

Here are the main problems encountered in selection interviewing:

- going into the interview 'cold' without reviewing job- or person-profiles and the applicant's documentation
- engaging in excessive chit-chat at the start of the interview. Polite pleasantries are all that is required
- failing to probe discrepancies or talk about sensitive issues because it may make the applicant or you feel uncomfortable
- being swayed by first impressions and by irrelevant and subjective data such as the physical attractiveness of the person (of either sex), their age, accent, social background and hobbies
- engaging in interview-speak. Interviewers often begin every question with 'Can you tell me . . .?' It soon grates!
- choosing too formal a seating arrangement, especially for panel interviews. It subdues conversation and reduces the chances of obtaining the information you want
- making verbatim notes; you cannot listen and write at the same time
- talking too much and listening too little

The following gameplan will help you avoid most of these problems.

1 Prepare

Preparation is vital. Your examination of the job- and person-profiles and of the application documentation (CV etc) will indicate which areas you should focus on, what information you need and how you will get it. Do this in advance! Reading through the application form during the interview is satisfactory neither for you nor for the applicant. Prepare thoroughly. If you do not you will probably fall back on subjective criteria. When it comes to preparing a job- and person-specification remember the findings of some recent research. It pointed to the fact that, often, the difference between an average performer and an excellent performer is often little to do with skill or technical knowledge but lies in the area of what one might call 'intangibles'. Attributes such as focus, flexibility, enthusiasm, adaptability, commitment, and energy are often where the key to superior performance lies. They can be difficult to uncover during a selection interview but you will still need to search for them.

To help, I use a three-column form containing details of the job, the person needed to fill it, and how I will uncover that information. This is shown in Table 5.14.

Table 5.14
Selection interview preparation form

Job title:

Job specification	Person specification	Information acquisition
What are the important activities, major challenges, and key characteristics of the job?	What are the competencies, characteristics and aptitudes of someone who will fit the job?	How will you find out if applicants 'fit the bill'? Will you find the information from their application form or CV, will you have to ask them in a way that does not indicate the answer you are looking for, or will a past employer be able to tell you?
How will customers (internal and external) judge the job-holder?	What must they be good at? What kind of personality traits must they have? What must they enjoy doing or not mind doing?	
Example: Computer Repair Engineer		
Solve technical computer problems.	Enthusiasm for solving computer problems.	See how applicant responds to technical-problem questions and to questions relating to most satisfying problems he/she has solved in the past.
Placate irate customers.	Good customer-handling skills.	Probe on relationships with existing customers; ask for examples of how he/she made customers happy; scenario questions on customer situations.
Call-out at unsocial hours.	Acceptance of unsocial hours.	Probe on repercussions of unsocial call-outs, out of work commitments etc. Check with current employer.

2 The welcome

The welcome should begin the moment the applicant responds to your advertisement. It should be evident in all correspondence and telephone contact. When they come for interview, reception should be expecting them. Any administrative matters such as travelling expenses, security photographs etc should be dealt with then, smoothly and efficiently. Receptionists should know if the current interview is overrunning and what to do about refreshments for the waiting applicant. The interview room should be 'shipshape' and you should be ready with all relevant documentation to hand.

3 The opening

First impressions matter and you only have one chance to make a good one – yes, you! If applicants are any good they will have more than one offer so you need to impress them sufficiently to accept yours. (Even if subsequently you do not want to offer them a job it is still good practice for them to leave the interview with a good impression.) Greet them with a smile, eye contact, and a warm handshake. Keep general chit-chat to a polite minimum (eg 'Did the information I sent arrive?', 'Did you find us all right?'). Contrary to popular belief, excessive chit-chat does not relax applicants. Explain who you are, how you would like to run the interview, and how long (roughly) it will take.

4 Obtain information

Obtain information before giving it. Some interviewers talk to alleviate their own nerves, some talk too much because they do not know any better, and some no doubt like the sound of their own voice. They give the applicant too much information at the beginning of the interview.

There are three main reasons for not beginning an interview by telling the applicant all about the company and the job for which they are applying. First, it can give bright applicants all the information they need to tailor what they say to fit your expectations, thereby reducing the quality of the information you obtain. For example: 'Now then, Mr Smith, this is a tough company: we've got too many people who think that work is some sort of restful activity they do between tea-breaks. We need tough managers to deal with skivers. So perhaps you'd like to tell me about your approach to management.' It is obvious what answer the interviewer wants to hear. Second, so much of your information may be new to the applicant that they will not remember it anyway. It will bore them. It certainly will not relax them. Finally, such an opening signals to them that you are the one doing the talking and their role is to shut up and listen.

Begin with 'safe' areas to encourage the applicant to 'loosen up', especially if their body language indicates nervousness. Begin with an *about* probe, such as an invitation to the applicant to tell you about a certain topic, in which they have maximum discretion about what to include. This type of probe is useful at the beginning of an interview when you want to discover the applicant's opinions, attitudes, or beliefs, or when you are unsure what to ask next but you do not want the momentum to 'stall'. It encourages the applicant to talk.

Then move to more significant areas. Remember that the applicant will probably have rehearsed answers to expected questions such as 'Why do you want to leave your current job?' and 'What attracted you to this vacancy?' Be prepared to probe and to ask the same question again in a different way. Probing is, without doubt, the most fertile ground for interviewers, yet it is also the area where most of the problems lie. So, remember the types of probe that are productive. They are listed here together with a few new ones especially useful in selection interviews.

Open probe: a question that cannot be answered with a simple yes or no, eg 'How do you feel about . . . ?', 'In what way?'.

Relevance probe: an open question designed to show how information fits together, eg 'How did you feel at the time?', 'What was the real outcome you wanted?' Such questions help you form 'patterns of understanding' and to test your assumptions about the applicant.

Closed probe: a question inviting a simple yes, no or some other specific answer.

Precise probe: a closed question asking for precision in the information supplied by the applicant, eg 'Which [noun] specifically?', 'How[verb] exactly?', 'Never?', 'In every case?' These are useful when you need more precise details on facts, actions etc, or when the applicant is using vague, general expressions such as 'everyone', 'they', 'better', 'more', 'less' etc.

Challenging probe: a question designed to make the applicant provide 'evidence', eg 'How much of that success was down to your efforts?' These probes are useful when the job profile demands an 'achiever' who should be able to stay calm under pressure, or where you suspect there has been exaggeration, eg 'That answer is inconsistent with the information on your CV. Would you clarify that, please?' or 'You're younger than the other candidates. How would you counter the suggestion that someone of your age may not have the life experience necessary for this post?'

Hypothetical probe: sometimes called a *scenario question*, this is a future-oriented question, eg 'What would you do if . . . ?', 'How would you handle . . . ?' It invites the applicant to describe how they would handle a given situation. The situation could be an example of 'real life' in the job or it could be an application of the 'principles' in a totally different setting. These questions are useful when you want to test how the applicant would react to or handle a situation without giving them any clues to the answer you are seeking. According to research, scenario questions have the same predictability as validated selection tests, yet are easy to administer. They also make the interview a satisfying experience for the applicant.

Pause: say nothing; use body language instead to encourage the applicant to continue talking. This can produce good results when someone is reluctant to talk.

Reflecting: this also helps a discussion to flow. It involves paraphrasing the last few words of the applicant, 'And you say you enjoyed it?'

It is worth remembering that the person asking the questions is in control of the pace and direction of a discussion, not the person doing the talking. Work on a 30:70 ratio of talking – 30 per cent from you and 70 per cent from the applicant. Think of the interview as a conversation with a purpose. This will make it easier for you to probe naturally rather than turn the interview into a question-and-answer session. It will also help you keep the atmosphere informal, which will give you the best chance of obtaining quality information. This is an approach to the interview where your listening skills are used to maximum capacity.

Here is a brief review: maintain helpful eye contact; look relaxed; lean slightly forward or slightly backward. Display encouraging responses – nodding, 'I see', etc. Ask relevant questions, make relevant comments, check your understanding, and summarise.

This is also an approach to the interview where the applicant's body language is likely to be most revealing. So watch for signs of tenseness, shyness, nervousness, vulnerability in response to a question, overconfidence, and lying. Another aspect of body language worth stressing for selection interviewers is *clusters of behaviour*. A hand-to-ear gesture on its own may mean nothing more than an itchy ear; but combined with a move to a more defensive and closed posture it may indicate that your question has touched a nerve and it is worth investigating further. Look for sudden changes of body language in relation to your questions, the information you are providing etc. Look for inconsistencies between what the applicant is saying with their mouth and what they are saying with their body.

Control your own body language, especially in response to unexpected answers. You want to give away as little in your reactions as poker players give away in theirs. You might also want to help relax the applicant by mirroring their body language – but do so subtly.

Do not make verbatim notes – jot down key words instead. When you do need to write something in detail, ask the applicant to hold on while you write it. Do not attempt to hide your notes. It is rude and will generate suspicion. Keep them in full view; all you are noting is what has been said, not what you think about it.

5 Give information

Whether or not the applicant has been asking questions as you have gone along it is good practice to offer them an opportunity to ask anything they wish. The type of questions they ask can also indicate a lot about their focus. For example, are they interested in facilities for smokers or in the computer system you use; in arrangements for paid overtime or in career progression; in fringe benefits or in what current employees do not like about the job?

6 Close professionally

The last impression is as important as the first one, so let the applicant know what will happen next and how long it will take; 'we'll let you know' sounds woolly compared to 'we'll finish interviews tomorrow and make a decision the day after. So you should have received a letter from us by the end of the week' – which sounds much more professional. Remember the smile and the eye contact as you shake hands.

Conclusion

Employing people is an expensive business and deserves to be carried out efficiently. Yet it is easy to miss vital information. Good interviews, however, can not only provide an accurate prediction of an applicant's suitability but also be a very enjoyable process for interviewer and applicant alike.

Table 5.15
Selecting the right candidate

1 **Prepare**	• Produce a three-column form showing job spec, person spec, and information-gathering strategy. • Read applicant's CV or application form.
2 **The welcome**	• Smile and make eye contact.
3 **The opening**	• Signpost format of interview.
4 **Obtain information**	• Use closed questions to check admin details; use 'about' probe to start off, then full range of probing tools; remember hypothetical probes especially productive. • Listen actively. • Pay close attention to applicant's body language. • Only key-word notes.
5 **Give information**	• Type of questions asked is further useful info.
6 **Close professionally**	• Give procedural details. • Smile and eye contact at close.

6

Implementation

Learning and then practising a new skill is a gratifying experience; transferring that skill to your job and to your life in general is an even more gratifying one! So now is the time to consider how you will implement what you have learnt. In this chapter we shall look at some ideas that people who have attended my courses have found helpful in implementing what they have learnt.

Attitude and problem definition

One of the obstacles to implementation is what goes on inside our heads. It is too easy to get into a habit of negative thinking which limits what we feel is possible. I would like therefore to introduce you to one of the most helpful positive-thinking techniques I have come across – 'circles of influence and concern'. They are described in detail in Stephen R. Covey's *The 7 Habits of Highly Effective People* (Hemel Hempstead, Simon & Schuster, 1992). I can most easily describe them with an example.

Let us consider a situation with which most of us are familiar – a bad day at work followed by a bad journey home in which a road-hog pulls out in front of us, dangerously and inconsiderately. We lose our temper, honk the horn, and flash our headlights. We also arrive home in a foul temper and, understandably, blame it on the road-hog: 'If only these road-hogs didn't get in my way, I'd still be in a good mood when I get home.' What we have done is to create a large gap between what concerns us (our mood when we get home) and what we can influence (the road-hogs).

What we need to do in order to put ourselves in control is re-define the problem. That is, we need to ensure that there is no gap, or only a small one, between what concerns us and what we can influence: 'If I can stay calm when these road-hogs get in my way, I'll still be in a good mood when I get home.' Figure 6.1 illustrates this.

Figure 6.1
Circles of influence and concern

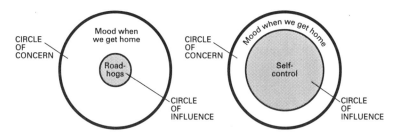

I have seen this approach change people's perspective on a problem from 'They're just not paying any attention to me' to 'I need to secure their attention, explain my case in terms they'll appreciate, and listen to their concerns.'

The effectiveness of the approach is that it puts you in control of yourself. Action is, after all, what counts, not sitting around complaining. It helps us take responsibility for what we want and, as such, it is an aid to positive thinking, stress management, and personal effectiveness. So, consider a situation that concerns you. How are you currently expressing your circles of influence and concern? How might you express them to bring them closer together?

Stepping-stones technique

Sometimes the size of a task can be very daunting. The gap between what we want to achieve with someone else and where we are now seems too huge to leap. My advice is: do not even try! Use stepping-stones instead.

The stepping-stones technique is a way of making large gaps easier to cross. All you have to do is take a problem one step at a time. Ask yourself, 'To remove this obstacle, what is the first thing I have to do, and the second, and the third, and so on?' For example, let us say that you want to stop Bill behaving a certain way towards you and that change is a big one to achieve; the stepping stones may look like Figure 6.2.

Figure 6.2
Stepping-stones technique – example

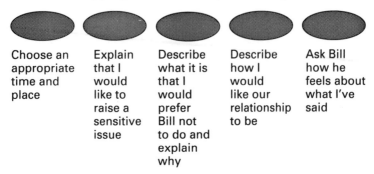

| Choose an appropriate time and place | Explain that I would like to raise a sensitive issue | Describe what it is that I would prefer Bill not to do and explain why | Describe how I would like our relationship to be | Ask Bill how he feels about what I've said |

Whatever the obstacle or task, this technique helps break it down into manageable proportions. It also helps you maintain an assertive mental attitude! What obstacles or tasks could you apply this technique to?

Mental dress rehearsals and mental replays

As I mentioned in the section on coaching, the mind is the key – so you might as well use it.

Our brains make little, if any, distinction between imagination and reality and you can use this facility in two ways. The first is to have a *mental dress rehearsal*. Think of a situation that is going to happen: imagine how you will open the conversation, how the other person will react, how good you will feel when you stay calm, and how you will use your core skills. This is as good as a real-life dress rehearsal – if not better, because you can make your imagination do anything you want. So when the situation arises in reality you have already experienced it and practised how you will handle it.

The second way to use this interplay between imagination and reality is to replay events that have already taken place. Not all situations give you time to prepare, and even when you *have* prepared, they do not always go the way you had hoped. So just like when you replay a video, you have a *mental replay* of the event to look at how you performed, what you did that helped, what you did that hindered, and how you would handle the situation differently next time. Then you can imagine the situation going exactly as you would have hoped. By the way, this is not idle fantasy. Top sportspeople have learnt the importance of a positive image about themselves and their ability. Many golfers, for example, having hit a bad shot, will imagine it going as they had intended before moving on, because that is the image they want to retain in their minds. If it helps them, it will help you too.

Help from your boss

Many managers are these days taking on the role of coach to their staff because they see the benefit not only to relationships but also to productivity in helping their people develop. Here are some suggestions on how, along with your boss, you can work on your influencing skills.

1 Prepare a summary of the key points of this book, what you have learnt from it, and how that will benefit your performance. Use no more than one side of A4 paper.
2 Discuss the summary with your boss as an introduction to your implementation plan.
3 Identify those aspects of your implementation plan that you would like your boss:
   - to help you with
   - to coach you on over a specified period
   - to agree specific goals on.
4 Agree with your boss specified review meetings (say, once a week for the first month and once a month for the next three months) during which you will:
   - discuss the progress of your implementation plan
   - review progress towards specific goals
   - set goals for the next review meeting.
5 Ask your boss to seek feedback from other people on how you are applying your influencing skills and to share it with you at the review meetings.

Your implementation plan

If this book is to be of real and lasting benefit you will need to determine what you intend to put into practice and how you intend to do it. You will find it helpful to:

- review the key points of each chapter.
- remind yourself of the argument behind each point.

For each point:

- Describe how it will benefit you.
- Outline what you will do to implement it.
- Identify what help you will need, and from whom.
- State a 'benchmark', that is describe the standard you will have reached when you have achieved your goal.
- State when you will start and give yourself a target date. Be specific – you will do x on a certain date, devote n hours each week to a specified item, or have performed a certain task by a given date.
- Specify a review date (or dates).
- Put appropriate entries in your diary.
- Copy the plan for your boss so that he or she can help.

Table 6.1 shows how you might wish to lay out your implementation plan.

Table 6.1
Implementation plan

Item	Benchmark	Time-scale	Review

7

A Few Final Thoughts

Let us begin this final chapter with a brief review. Here are the main points I have made in this book.

- Behaviour is the inescapable link between our intentions and the results we actually achieve. In order to achieve what we intend to achieve we need to be skilled in both *what* we do and in *how* we do it. Because much of what we achieve is with or through other people, interpersonal skills are essential.
- There are only a few interpersonal skills. In the same way as a cook will use the same basic ingredients to create a variety of dishes we can mix together our core skills in different ways depending on the situation we are in.
- Interpersonal skills can be used manipulatively or positively. Using them positively produces better results. Using them positively means recognising five fundamental principles that relate to influencing people. The principles recognise that people have rights.
- A positive approach to influencing other people is a workplace necessity because of current changes in the world of work. We are undergoing a social revolution affecting the way people at work relate to one another. To be effective in that environment you will need positive influencing skills.

In making these points I have explained what the five fundamental principles are (see Chapter 2). I have described the five core skills (see Chapter 3). I have shown how those skills can be combined into gameplans for a variety of situations (see Chapters 4 and 5). I have given you some suggestions which, I hope, will help you implement what you have learnt so that you benefit at work from having read this book (see Chapter 6). But I would like you to benefit still further. I would like to sow a seed of thought in your mind. It concerns what you will do with your positive influencing skills outside work. Let me explain with a short story.

I recall attending a course on customer care many years ago. The presenter made the point that if we had taken his messages to heart and were about to meet a customer, we would think of what we could do to make that customer glad they were dealing with us. He then asked us how we could transfer the principles to other aspects of our lives. What would we do, for example, that evening to make our families glad we had arrived home?

I do not think many people in the audience had thought of that until he mentioned it. We seem not to think about how what we learn in one aspect of our lives can be transferred to another. How many accountants, for example, produce ratio figures for their domestic accounts? How many people, having learnt about objective setting, set objectives for their private, as opposed to work, lives? How many people who attend coaching courses start coaching their children?

Children are probably a good example. When you consider that most of life's problems stem from other people, then if children are taught positive influencing skills at an early age maybe they will grow up better able to cope with what life will throw at them. That is probably the most precious gift a parent can give a child.

I would like to share two examples with you that involve my own children. The first concerns my daughter, Alex. At the time of this anecdote she had a friend whose house backed onto the local common. The friend would often want Alex to go for a walk onto the common when they were, in my opinion, too young to be out unsupervised. The friend was fiercely independent and very persuasive, and would use the usual manipulation techniques that kids are so good at to try to get her way. When I heard about this I taught Alex the 'broken record' technique, which we role-played. The next conversation between the two girls went something like this:

- C'mon, Alex, let's go for a walk over the common.
- I don't want to. I'd rather play in the garden.
- You're not scared, are you?
- No, I just don't want to go over the common.
- But no one will know.
- Maybe they won't but I still don't want to go.
- You're just being selfish.

– I'd just rather stay in the garden.
– What's the matter? Aren't you my friend any more?
– Yes, I want to play with you. I just don't want to go over the common.
– Oh all right then, we'll play in the garden.

No feelings of guilt, shame, or awkwardness on Alex's part – just a simple standing-up for her rights.

In the second example my son, Edward, displayed fine inter-personal skills – at the age of seven! It happened that I was collecting him from school one day. I was in a hurry and wanted to get back home quickly. He was late but eventually, and a bit impatiently, I got him out of the classroom, across the playground, and into the car. As we were buckling our seat-belts he told me that he had forgotten one of his books. So we had to get out of the car, lock the doors, go back into the school, across the playground, and into his classroom to retrieve it, then out of the classroom etc, etc back to the car. As we pulled away I did the usual 'impatient Dad' stuff, telling Edward he ought to take more care, and that we were now even later and a few other choice remarks besides. By this time we were about a quarter of a mile from the school. He then said very quietly, 'Dad, there's something else . . . and it's going to bother you.' I asked him what. 'I've forgotten my spelling book and I need it tonight.'

We drove back to the school and, after we had parked, I told Edward that he had just done two things of which I was immensely proud. First, despite being afraid that I would lose my temper at yet another delay, he had done what he needed to do. That was brave. Second, he had done some of the neatest sign-posting I had seen for a long time. That was good because it got my attention and prepared me for what he had to say. I also confessed to feeling bad about my previous demonstration of impatience, and I thanked him for being sensible enough for the both of us – all this was said with eye contact and pause, as you would expect in a good praising.

Having good interpersonal skills is however only part of the story. Skills such as these emanate from as well as help develop a robust self-esteem, which I believe to be essential for a fulfilling life. I also find it fun having coaching sessions with my kids; I hope it makes up a bit for the times when I am as tired, grumpy, and impatient as any other father. I also hope that if I listen to them when they are six, they will listen to me when they are 16.

What will you do with your positive influencing skills? Will you use them to get on better with that difficult neighbour; to ensure that the garage carries out the service properly this time; or to finish the next meeting of the Parent–Teacher Association in record time?

With whom will you share the skills? Your children, your spouse or partner, fellow social club committee members?

I believe it makes sense to spread the word. The more people who adopt positive influencing skills, based on the five fundamental principles, the more likely we are to listen to one another, to seek to understand one another, and to try to make ourselves understood. We will seek to do all this openly and honestly, without manipulation. That has to be right. It passes my TSR Test. I hope it passes yours.

When I run a course I like to encourage feedback from participants, and that is a principle I would like to extend to readers of this book. So if you wish to comment on what you have read or, even better, describe how it may have helped you, do please contact me:

Terry Gillen Training
PO Box 585
Tring
Hertfordshire, HP23 5BD
England
Tel/Fax 01442–891527

Further Reading

Further reading is an excellent way to maintain your interest in, and improve your knowledge of, a subject; here then is a selection of books that you may find useful.

GILLEN T. *Assertiveness for Managers*. Aldershot, Gower, 1992
A thorough text explaining in detail what assertiveness is and how it applies to a variety of situations that managers and other people find themselves in. As one reviewer put it, 'You ought to read this. No. Try again. There are messages here you cannot afford to miss.'

HONEY P. *Improve Your People Skills*. London, IPM, 1988
—— *Problem People . . . and how to manage them*. London, IPD 1992
—— *Solving People-problems*. Maidenhead, McGraw-Hill, 1980
The first book is a good A–Z of all things interpersonal, while the second is an A–Z guide to handling problem people; the third explains what behaviour modification is and how to use it.

HARRIS T. A. *I'm OK – You're OK*. London, Pan Books, 1973
A standard textbook on transactional analysis, providing insights into how we interact with others and why we communicate the way we do.

PALLADINO C. D. *Developing Self-esteem*. London, Kogan Page, 1990
GELLMAN M. and GAGE D. *Improve Your Confidence Quotient*. London, Thorsons, 1987
Two interesting and easy-to-read books on self-esteem.

COVEY S. R. *7 Habits of Highly Effective People*. Hemel Hempstead, Simon & Schuster, 1992

This is subtitled 'Powerful lessons in personal change' – and deservedly so. A very thorough work based on simple but fundamental principles.

BLANCHARD K. and JOHNSON S. *The One Minute Manager*. London, Fontana, 1983
BLANCHARD K. and LORBER R. *Putting the One Minute Manager to Work*. London, Fontana/Collins, 1984
Entertaining and easy-to-read books on establishing and reviewing performance standards.

WHITMORE J. *Coaching for Performance*. London, Nicholas Brealey, 1992
Thorough, easy-to-read, and practical advice from an acknowledged expert.

DE BONO E. *Six Thinking Hats*. London, Penguin, 1990
A book by the inventor of lateral thinking that shows how our thoughts get out of synchronisation in meetings and suggests what to do about it.

PEASE A. *Body Language*. London, Sheldon Press, 1981
A well-presented, fully illustrated, and useful book on the subject.

Index

appraisal, 46, 137–42
arguments, stacking up 105
assertiveness 37–8, 92–102, 115
assertiveness techniques 96–100
assumptions 24
attitudes 10, 206–07
authority at work 5

bad news, giving 161–6
behaviour *viii*, 11, 24–9, 33, 150,
   151–2
  counter-productive 13–14
behaviour modification 27
beliefs 10, 11, 31–2
benefits 17
Blanchard, K. et al 148–9
body language 37, 76–92, 114–15
  and culture 79
  eyes 80–81
  gestures 85–7
  posture 82–4
  proximity 84–5
  voice 81–2
Bono, Edward de 60
boss, help from 209
brain 28
'broken record' 97–9

Carlisle, John 74
children 212–14
circles of influence and concern
   206–07
coaching 43, 45, 166–75
'command and control' structure *viii*
common vision 17
compulsory competitive tendering 2
consequence, pointing out a 99–100
contracting out 2
core skills 36–135, 117–35, 136
cost leadership 2

counselling 156–61
counter-proposals 104
Covey, Stephen 206
credibility, personal 6–7
criticism, constructive *see* reprimanding
customer care 2, 5, 8

defend/attack spirals 104–05
de-layering *viii*
delays, handling people who cause
  you 174–8
difference of opinion, resolving a
  183–8
disagreement 55
discrepancy, pointing out a 99

emotive language 57–8
empowerment 2, 8
evaluating 40, 158

feedback, giving *see* appraisal
fight or flight 92–3
formalspeak 106–07
formative years 31

gameplans 136–205
Gore, W. & Associates 4–5
group discussions *see* meetings

Hemery, David 170
hierarchy, organisational 5–7, 30–31
Honey, Peter 27
Huthwaite Research Group 16

implementation 206–10
implementation plan 210
information, filtering of 52
interpreting 40, 41, 158
involvement 16–19, 33

knowledge, technical 6–7

labels, labelling 24–5, 29
listening 36, 48–51, 114
   active 49–51
   passive 51
logic, spurious 22–3, 113

manager's insurance policy 173–4
manipulation 19–24, 101
   and how to resist it 108–13
   best offer 109
   feeling guilty/responsible 111–12
   principal ploy 110
   subsidiary decision 110–11
   spurious logic 113
Margerison, Charles 17, 144
market testing 2
matrix teams 2
meetings 58–60
   productive 194–8
mental dress rehearsals 208–09
mental replays 208–09

negotiating 177–83
Nissan UK 3
no-noes 102–07, 115
non-verbal communication see body
   language

order fodder 4

packaging 151–2
parents 23, 93
pause 44
Pease, Allan 91
personality 11
persuasion 10, 19–24, 33, 187–94
Peters, Tom 5
praise, contaminated 144
praising 143–8
principles, fundamental 10–35
probing 36, 38–48, 113
process manager 60
public sector 2
pull/pulling 10–11, 12–16, 33

question
   closed 44
   evaluative 48
   forced choice 46–7
   hypothetical 42, 75
   leading 47
   open 39
   reflective 39
   scenario see hypothetical
   and signposting 56

Rackham, Neil 16, 74
ratio of talking 19
recognition capacity of the brain 28,
   52
red-rag words and phrases 103–04
re-engineering 2
reflecting 40, 41
reprimanding 148–56
revolution 1
Roger, Carl 40
'royal we' 105–06

sales pitch 68
seeking information 74
selection interview 42, 45, 198–205
self-disclosure 56–7, 75
self-esteem 149–50
selling
   facts of life 61–3
   persuasive 37, 61–74, 114
   sequence 64–7
Semler, Ricardo 4–5
signposting 53–5, 75
solution-oriented influencing 75–6
stepping-stone technique 207–08
Steve Davis principle vii–viii
submissive behaviour 94
sympathising 40, 41

thinking pattern 52
tolerance 101
total quality management 2, 3, 5, 8
transactional analysis 150–51
triggers and responses 25–8, 95–6
TSR test viii–ix, 33, 214

understanding/being understood
29–32, 33, 55, 74

values 10
verbal reasoning ability 93

wavelength 37, 52–61, 114
Whitacker, David 170
Whitmore, John 170